MW00896789

TERRORIST FINANCING: KIDNAPPING, ANTIQUITIES TRAFFICKING, AND PRIVATE DONATIONS

HEARING

BEFORE THE

SUBCOMMITTEE ON TERRORISM, NONPROLIFERATION, AND TRADE

OF THE

COMMITTEE ON FOREIGN AFFAIRS HOUSE OF REPRESENTATIVES

ONE HUNDRED FOURTEENTH CONGRESS

FIRST SESSION

NOVEMBER 17, 2015

Serial No. 114–120

Printed for the use of the Committee on Foreign Affairs

Available via the World Wide Web: http://www.foreignaffairs.house.gov/ or
http://www.gpo.gov/fdsys/

U.S. GOVERNMENT PUBLISHING OFFICE

97–635PDF   WASHINGTON : 2015

For sale by the Superintendent of Documents, U.S. Government Publishing Office
Internet: bookstore.gpo.gov   Phone: toll free (866) 512–1800; DC area (202) 512–1800
Fax: (202) 512–2104   Mail: Stop IDCC, Washington, DC 20402–0001

COMMITTEE ON FOREIGN AFFAIRS

EDWARD R. ROYCE, California, *Chairman*

CHRISTOPHER H. SMITH, New Jersey
ILEANA ROS-LEHTINEN, Florida
DANA ROHRABACHER, California
STEVE CHABOT, Ohio
JOE WILSON, South Carolina
MICHAEL T. McCAUL, Texas
TED POE, Texas
MATT SALMON, Arizona
DARRELL E. ISSA, California
TOM MARINO, Pennsylvania
JEFF DUNCAN, South Carolina
MO BROOKS, Alabama
PAUL COOK, California
RANDY K. WEBER SR., Texas
SCOTT PERRY, Pennsylvania
RON DeSANTIS, Florida
MARK MEADOWS, North Carolina
TED S. YOHO, Florida
CURT CLAWSON, Florida
SCOTT DesJARLAIS, Tennessee
REID J. RIBBLE, Wisconsin
DAVID A. TROTT, Michigan
LEE M. ZELDIN, New York
DANIEL DONOVAN, New York

ELIOT L. ENGEL, New York
BRAD SHERMAN, California
GREGORY W. MEEKS, New York
ALBIO SIRES, New Jersey
GERALD E. CONNOLLY, Virginia
THEODORE E. DEUTCH, Florida
BRIAN HIGGINS, New York
KAREN BASS, California
WILLIAM KEATING, Massachusetts
DAVID CICILLINE, Rhode Island
ALAN GRAYSON, Florida
AMI BERA, California
ALAN S. LOWENTHAL, California
GRACE MENG, New York
LOIS FRANKEL, Florida
TULSI GABBARD, Hawaii
JOAQUIN CASTRO, Texas
ROBIN L. KELLY, Illinois
BRENDAN F. BOYLE, Pennsylvania

AMY PORTER, *Chief of Staff*   THOMAS SHEEHY, *Staff Director*
JASON STEINBAUM, *Democratic Staff Director*

———

SUBCOMMITTEE ON TERRORISM, NONPROLIFERATION, AND TRADE

TED POE, Texas, *Chairman*

JOE WILSON, South Carolina
DARRELL E. ISSA, California
PAUL COOK, California
SCOTT PERRY, Pennsylvania
REID J. RIBBLE, Wisconsin
LEE M. ZELDIN, New York

WILLIAM KEATING, Massachusetts
BRAD SHERMAN, California
BRIAN HIGGINS, New York
JOAQUIN CASTRO, Texas
ROBIN L. KELLY, Illinois

CONTENTS

TERRORIST FINANCING: KIDNAPPING, ANTIQUITIES TRAFFICKING, AND PRIVATE DONATIONS

TUESDAY, NOVEMBER 17, 2015

HOUSE OF REPRESENTATIVES,
SUBCOMMITTEE ON TERRORISM, NONPROLIFERATION, AND TRADE,
COMMITTEE ON FOREIGN AFFAIRS,
Washington, DC.

The subcommittee met, pursuant to notice, at 2 o'clock p.m., in room 2200 Rayburn House Office Building, Hon. Ted Poe (chairman of the subcommittee) presiding.

Mr. POE. The subcommittee is called to order.

Without objection, all members may have 5 days to submit statements, questions, extraneous materials for the record subject to the length limitation in the rules.

The Chair recognizes itself for an opening statement and when the ranking member, Mr. Keating, gets here he will be, of course, allowed to make his opening statement. But we will proceed at this time.

The terrorist attacks in Paris last Friday remind us the damage a terrorist organization can do with even a little money. ISIS, however, is the richest terrorist organization in history.

Last year alone, ISIS made over $1 billion. That is more money than some countries make in a year. Much of that money was made from seizing state assets, selling oil on the black market and taxing people living in its so-called caliphate.

Those sources of money are mostly internal and do not use the international financial system. But other sources of funding are more dependent on the outside world and may be easier to cut off.

For example, ISIS made nearly $50 million last year from kidnapping for ransom. Some estimates put kidnapping for ransom as high as 20 percent of ISIS' revenue.

ISIS is not the only terrorist group kidnapping hostages to make money. AQIM is said to rely almost exclusively on kidnapping for ransom for funds.

This is the same terrorist group that attacked a gas plant in Algeria and killed one of my constituents, Victor Lovelady, after taking him hostage.

From 2008 to 2014, terrorist groups made roughly $165 million from ransom payments. To try and stop this wave of payments in the last 2 years the United Nations passed three Security Council resolutions condemning the payment of ransoms to terrorists.

Our own country has a long history of countering this barbaric practice. From the very beginning, the United States has always refused to pay ransom to terrorists.

The Barbary Pirates captured American merchant ships and demanded ransoms to release the crews in the early 1800s. Even then, President Thomas Jefferson refused to pay the bounty.

Jefferson argued that doing so would only encourage more attacks. Throughout history, terrorists have learned to demand ransoms from those who will pay.

Also, I want to recognize that this issue can be complex. We have the mother of James Foley here with us today. Mrs. Foley, I want to express my condolences to you for the loss of your son.

I think it is important that we hear from family members of those who are kidnapped so I appreciate—the committee appreciates the fact that you were willing to testify.

Terrorist groups have long depended on criminal activity for funding including trafficking of cultural antiquities. ISIS is currently in control of hundreds of sites throughout Syria and Iraq.

These sites are the cultural heritage of humanity but ISIS sees them as a financial opportunity. Declassified ISIS documents show that the terrorists made hundreds of millions of dollars from selling these antiquities.

According to some estimates, antiquity smuggling at one point was ISIS' second largest source of funding. ISIS is killing people with the money it makes from these artifacts while also destroying history.

Believe it or not, there are some people who voluntarily give their money to these murderers. ISIS has maintained connections with wealthy donors for nearly a decade. Many of these donors are based in Gulf countries like Qatar, Kuwait and Saudi Arabia.

Between 2013 and 2014, ISIS received as much as $40 million from these wealthy benefactors, and ISIS is not the only terrorist group benefitting from these deep pocket donors who give money to terrorist groups.

Wealthy individuals from these countries fund terrorists all over the world including al-Qaeda and Al-Shabaab. They set up charities and funnel the money directly to the terrorists.

The governments of these Gulf countries simply do not do enough to stop the steady stream of terrorist financing that seems to start from a handful of Middle Eastern countries.

These private donors are just as guilty as the terrorists. Unless more is done, the governments of these countries are complicit in the crimes.

These three sources of terrorist funding have given ISIS hundreds of millions of dollars in the last year. Cutting off even one of these sources could make a big difference. ISIS thrives off the appearance that it is winning.

By cutting even a portion of ISIS' funds we can challenge its narrative of victory. That will mean not only less money for the terrorists but also possibly less recruits.

More importantly, it would mean less victims of ISIS' barbaric terrorist attacks. We must use all the resources at our disposal to target every source of terrorist funding no matter where it comes from and that is the purpose of these hearings to listen to these experts on this issue.

I will now turn to the gentleman from Massachusetts for his opening statement, Mr. Keating.

Mr. KEATING. Thank you, Mr. Chairman.

Thank you for conducting this hearing. Thank you to our witnesses for being here today. This hearing is on terrorist financing generally but in consideration of the recent events it is an opportunity and an appropriate one to pay particular attention to ISIL.

Friday's attack in Paris and recent bombings in Beirut, the bombing, we can now say, of the Russian passenger Metrojet in Egypt indicate that ISIL may intend increasingly to attack targets outside of its basis of power in Iraq and Syria and it is worth taking a moment to express on behalf of myself and I think the committee, you know, our greatest sympathy for the victims and their families of those terrible tragedies.

This worrisome development in the United States and our allies must endeavor at all fronts—demonstrates we must endeavor on all fronts to defeat ISIL.

In order to defeat ISIL, we need to continue to assist our allies militarily to roll back the territorial gains made by ISIL and in addition and not unimportantly we must work to cut off ISIL's supply of money and manpower by more effectively countering terrorist recruitment, terrorist travel and terrorist financing.

According to a 2015 report by the Financial Action Task Force, ISIL earns revenue from several sources including various illicit proceeds derived from the occupation of territory, kidnapping for ransom, donations by or through nonprofit organizations, support from foreign fighters, and fund-raising through the Internet.

One of the significant ways ISIL finances its activities is through the illicit sale of antiquities. ISIL is directly involved in the lootings of archeological sites in Iraq and Syria, theft from regional museums and stockpiling of cultural objects for future sale on the international market.

Further, ISIL earns money by charging others for licenses they call taxes to loot archeological sites and by taxing traffickers moving items through ISIL-controlled territory.

To date, ISIL has reportedly earned tens of millions of dollars from the antiquities stolen in Syria alone. To counter this threat, we need to do more to prevent the theft and destruction of antiquities in countries like Iraq and Syria.

We also need to do more here at home to ensure that the United States isn't importing stolen antiquities and financing terrorism as a result.

I have introduced the bill H.R. 2285, the Prevent Trafficking in Cultural Properties Act, that would enhance coordination and training within the Department of Homeland Security to stop stolen antiquities from entering the United States and, even more importantly, to investigate and then prosecute the smugglers, traffickers and other criminals that participate in this illicit trade.

H.R. 2285 was recently reported out of the Committee on Homeland Security and I urge my colleagues to support this bipartisan bill, which is aimed at stopping terrorist groups like ISIL from fi-

4

nancing the murderous activities through the sale of stolen antiquities and other cultural property.

I look forward to hearing from our witnesses today and learning more about different forms of terrorist financing including antiquities trafficking and how better to stop this illicit stream of income.

Thank you, Mr. Chairman. I yield back.

Mr. POE. I thank the gentleman from Massachusetts.

The Chair will now recognize members who wish to make opening statements for 1 minute each.

Chair recognizes the gentleman from California, Mr. Cook, for 1 minute in his opening statement.

Mr. COOK. Thank you, Mr. Chairman.

This is certainly a very timely hearing. I want to thank Ms. Foley for being here. This past week many of us gave speeches, talked about Veterans Day and the sacrifice that so many Americans have given in wars.

And no matter how you slice it, this is a war that we are waging with this group—ISIL, ISIS, Daesh, whatever you want to call them.

Their tactics—you know, there are no limits to them and I personally think that many people in the Middle East and throughout the world have gotten a pass on this.

We know that there has been support of that through some nations in the Middle East, the Gulf States—a lot of money, all these different things that has already been mentioned by my colleagues.

But without a doubt, we have to do something about this and I think this, as I said, after what happened it is the most timely hearing we could have on the Hill.

Thank you.

Mr. POE. I thank the gentleman.

The Chair wants to recognize the gentleman from New York, Mr. Higgins, and also I recognize the work that he is doing on the issue of kidnapping of Americans for ransom.

So the gentleman from New York is recognized.

Mr. HIGGINS. Thank you, Chairman Poe. Thank you for holding this, obviously, important and timely hearing.

Kidnapping for ransom, antiquity smuggling and private donations represent an alarming and largely under appreciated source of terrorist financing that has largely gone unaddressed.

Further complicating our counter financing efforts, many of these transactions are conducted without reliance on the international banking system, rendering many of our tools such as sanctions and terrorist designations ineffective.

In recent years, kidnapping for ransom has become an increasingly lucrative enterprise with reports indicating as much as $165 million has been paid to al-Qaeda and ISIS since 2008 for the return of hostages.

Unlike the United States and United Kingdom, many of our allies continue to pay ransoms, resulting in a vicious cycle in which terrorist groups specifically seek out citizens of countries known to pay, resulting in more kidnappings.

We must ensure our friends and allies halt government-sponsored ransom payments. Doing so will lead to fewer kidnappings while also depriving terrorists of a major revenue source.

I am pleased to be working closely with Chairman Poe to develop legislation to address this issue and I look forward to today's witnesses and I yield back the balance of my time.

Mr. POE. I thank the gentleman from New York.

The Chair now recognizes the gentleman from South Carolina, Mr. Wilson.

Mr. WILSON. Thank you, Mr. Chairman, for your leadership on this critical issue of terrorist financing.

I would like to extend my sincerest appreciation to Ms. Foley for the courage that you have shown in coming before the committee today to share your story. Our hearts truly are with you and your family.

The murderous attacks in Paris killing 159 citizens on Friday, the Beirut killing of 41 persons last week and the bombing of the Russian charter jet killing 224 innocent passengers October 31st further highlight the fact that our current methods of preventing Daesh ISIL's terror financing are not working.

It is critical that America and its allies have the necessary resources to cut off ISIL's funding from any source that we can.

It is imperative that those who do business or provide funding to the Islamic State in any way are able to be accurately identified and that we have laws in place to deal with them.

I look forward to the recommendations of the panel.

Mr. POE. Do any other members wish to be recognized for an opening statement?

Therefore, without objection all members will have 5 days to submit statements, questions, extraneous materials for the record subject to the length limitation in the rules.

And also without objection, all the witness' prepared statements will be made part of the record. I ask that each witness please keep your presentation to no more than 5 minutes. I will introduce each witness and then give him time for their comments.

Mr. John Cassara is a formal special agent to the U.S. Department of Treasury's Office of Terrorism and Financial Intelligence. Mr. Cassara is considered an expert in money laundering in the Middle East and the growing threat of alternative remittance systems.

Dr. David Weinberg is a senior fellow at the Foundation for Defense of Democracies where he worked primarily on Saudi Arabia and the Gulf States.

His research in this area focuses on energy security, counter terrorism, alliance transparency and human rights.

Ms. Diane Foley is the mother of James Foley, an American journalist who was kidnapped and killed by ISIS last year.

She is the founder of James Foley Legacy Foundation to continue James' legacy of freedom and justice for those without a voice, and once again, Ms. Foley, thank you very much for being here today.

Dr. Michael Danti currently serves as the academic director of the American Schools of Oriental Research Cultural Heritage Initiatives, which monitors and reports on the heritage situation in Syria and northern Iraq.

He is a Near Eastern archeologist with experience directing programs in Syria, Iraq and Iran.

Mr. Cassara, we will start with you and you have 5 minutes.

STATEMENT OF MR. JOHN CASSARA (FORMER SPECIAL AGENT, U.S. DEPARTMENT OF THE TREASURY)

Mr. CASSARA. Chairman Poe and members of the subcommittee, thank you for the opportunity to testify today. It is an honor for me to be here.

Mr. Chairman, I have submitted a written statement. I would like to take just a few minutes to give a brief summary.

Kidnapping for ransom is a crime as old as antiquity. Unfortunately, in recent years, terrorists and associated criminal organizations have turned to kidnapping as a relatively easy and lucrative source of funding.

The United Nations' estimates that approximately $120 million in ransom payments was paid to terrorist groups between 2004 and 2012. Some experts believe kidnapping for ransom is our most significant terrorist financing threat today.

As the tragic events in Paris last Friday make clear, the United States and the international community are rightfully alarmed about ISIS.

The terror organization has kidnapped multi hundreds if not thousands of victims including local Iraqis, Syrians, members of ethnic minorities as well as Westerners and other foreign nationals living in the region.

Some were brutally murdered to send a political message. Others were used to extract ransom payments. According to the Financial Action Task Force, in 2014 ISIS raised approximately $45 million from kidnapping for ransom.

In fact, because kidnapping and associated crimes such as extortion have been so successful, it appears the average ransom payment is increasing. It is a vicious cycle.

There is no doubt that ransom payments lead to future kidnappings, and future kidnappings lead to additional ransom payments and, of course, the ransom payments eventually build the capacity of terrorist organizations which fuels additional terrorist attacks.

There have been several United Nation Security Council resolutions attempting to curtail ransom payments into terrorist organizations' coffers. Despite the restrictions, the world has not stopped payment.

Of course, the complicating factor is our humanity. It is difficult to turn away from the anguished cries of those kidnapped and the frantic appeals of those—of their loved ones.

Last week, a new book that I wrote was released, "Trade-Based Money Laundering: The Next Frontier in International Money Laundering Enforcement."

It is often overlooked but the misuse of trade and associated underground financial systems are often part of the kidnap for ransom equation.

For example, money and value transfer services are found throughout Iraq and Syria, including areas where ISIS operates. Sometimes they are called hawaladars. They are trusted brokers and have established relationships throughout the region. They operate on trust and secrecy.

Hawaladars generally do not conduct electronic fund transfers as banks do but rather communicate via email, fax and phone with a local or foreign associate to pay or receive payment from a counter party to the transaction.

Eventually brokers have to settle their accounts. Sometimes they use cash, sometimes the conventional banking system.

But I want to emphasize and something that is continually overlooked and that is historically and culturally in all areas of the world where terrorist adversaries opposite, trade-based value transfer is used to balance the books or settle accounts.

So examining trade records for invoice fraud and value transfer could be the back door into money and value transfer systems used by terrorists.

Unfortunately, neither the United States nor partners are doing this. Moreover, I can make the argument that if one includes all its varied forms including underground financial systems, trade-based money laundering could very well be the largest money laundering methodology in the world and unfortunately it is also the least understood, recognized and enforced.

Yet, I am optimistic. By using modern analytic tools to exploit a variety of relevant big data sets, I believe international trade transparency is theoretically achievable or certainly possible to factor many times over what we have today.

As an added bonus, cracking down on trade fraud could also be a significant revenue enhancer for the governments involved.

In my book and written statement I go into detail on many of these issues and I provide a number of recommendations on achieving trade transparency so as to combat trade-based money laundering, underground finance and terror.

I appreciate the opportunity to appear before you today and I am happy to answer any questions you may have.

Thank you.

[The prepared statement of Mr. Cassara follows:]

Trade Based Money Laundering
John Cassara

John A. Cassara

Former Intelligence Officer and Treasury Special Agent

Hearing on

"Terrorist Funding: Kidnapping for Ransom, Antiquities, and Private Donors"

Before the Terrorism, Nonproliferation, and Trade Subcommittee

of the

House Foreign Affairs Committee

November 17, 2015

Chairman Poe and Members of the Subcommittee on Terrorism, Nonproliferation and Trade;

Thank you for the opportunity to testify today. It is an honor for me to be here.

I retired after a 26 year career as a Case Officer for the Central Intelligence Agency and as a Special Agent for the U.S. Department of Treasury. I believe I am the only individual to have ever been both a covert Case Officer and a Treasury Special Agent.

Much of my career with Treasury was involved with combating international money laundering and terror finance. Since my retirement, I have been a contractor and consultant for a number of U.S. departments, agencies, and business enterprises. I have been fortunate to continue my domestic and international travels primarily providing training and technical assistance in financial crimes enforcement. I have written four books on money laundering and terror finance as well as numerous published articles. Additional information can be found on my website: www.JohnCassara.com

• • • • • • • • • • •

"Without money, there is no terrorism."

This simple truism was recognized early on. A few days after the deadliest terrorist attack in U.S. history, President George W. Bush stated, "Money is the lifeblood of terrorist operations. Today we are asking the world to stop payment."

More than 14 years after the September 11 attacks, we are meeting here this afternoon in part to ask, "Has President Bush's original request been fulfilled? Has the world stopped payment?

Of course, the answer is not simple. Successful terrorist and organized criminal groups diversify their funding sources. Similarly, they diversify the ways they launder their money. Our adversaries are creative and they adapt.

This afternoon, I would like to talk about an increasingly troublesome source of funding – kidnapping, ransom and extortion sometimes known by its acronym KRE.

I would then like to briefly discuss two other related money laundering and terror finance methodologies: trade-based money laundering (TBML) and underground financial systems. Both are loosely tied to KRE.

Kidnapping for ransom is a crime as old as antiquity. In recent years, terrorist and associated organized criminal organizations have turned to kidnapping as a relatively easy and lucrative source of funding. The United Nations feels the problem is growing. The UN estimates that approximately $120 million in ransom payments was paid to terrorist groups alone between 2004 and 2012.[i] And according to a 2012 assessment by David S. Cohen, the Treasury Under Secretary for Terrorism and Finance Intelligence, kidnapping for ransom is our most significant terrorist financing threat today.[ii]

In 2014, 35 percent of kidnappings were in Asia, followed by Africa at 30 percent, the Americas with 21 percent, the Middle East with 12 percent and Europe/Russia with 2 percent.[iii]

We are all concerned about the growth and savagery of the Islamic State of Iraq and the Levant (ISIS). The terror organization has kidnapped multi-hundreds if not thousands of victims, including local Iraqis, Syrians and members of ethnic minorities, as well as Westerners, and East Asians located in the region. Some were used to extract ransom payments, and others were brutally murdered to send a political message. Because kidnapping is both profitable and valuable as a propaganda tool, ISIS has reportedly purchased Western hostages from moderate rebels at border exchanges. According to a Financial Action Task Force (FATF) assessment, in 2014 ISIS raised approximately $20 - $45 million from kidnapping for ransom.[iv]

Foreign nationals taken hostage worldwide vary from aid workers to tourists, from employees of private companies to diplomats or other government officials. Americans are not immune. Although an estimated 60 – 70 percent of overseas kidnapping of U.S. citizens goes unreported, last year, according to the Bureau of Consular Affairs at the State Department, more than two dozen Americans working in private industry were kidnapped in terrorism-related incidents.[v]

Demands may also be evolving beyond ransoms to extortion and protection money. One Al-Qaeda affiliate was planning to extort substantial annual payments, amounting to millions of euros a year, from a European-based company, in exchange for a promise not to target that company's interests in Africa. And extortion is[vi] often used by terrorist groups in the extraction industry such as oil and minerals, agriculture, various production facilities, cultural artefacts, etc.

In Southeast Asia, piracy at sea is reaching record levels.[vii] By using tactics such as extortion and shakedowns, terrorist organizations are following the playbook of organized crime.

Because kidnapping and associated crimes have been so successful, it appears the average ransom payment is increasing. It is a vicious cycle. There is no doubt that ransom payments lead to future kidnappings, and future kidnappings lead to additional ransom payments. And, of course, the ransom payments build the capacity of terrorist organizations which in turn fuels additional terrorist attacks.

Logically, we must do what President Bush urged: "Ask the world to stop payment."

To this end, there have been several United Nations Security Council Resolutions (UNSCRs), including 2133 (2014) and 2170 (2014) that call on member states to prevent terrorists from benefitting, directly or indirectly from ransom payments. UNSCR 2161 (2014) confirms that the prohibition on providing funds to individuals and entities on the al-Qaida Sanctions List, including ISIS, also applies to the payment of ransoms to individuals, groups, or entities on the list, regardless of how or by whom the ransom is paid. Thus 2161 applies to both direct and indirect ransom payments through multiple intermediaries. The restrictions cover not only the ultimate payer of the ransom, but also the parties that may mediate such transfers, including insurance companies, consultancies, and any other financial facilitators.[viii]

Despite the restrictions, the world has not stopped payment. Reportedly, even some governments have rewarded terrorists with ransom payments. But of course, the complicating factor is our humanity. It is difficult to turn away from the anguished cries of those kidnapped and the frantic appeals of their loved ones.

ISIS, Al-Qaeda in the Lands of the Islamic Maghreb (AQIM), Al-Qaeda in the Arabian Peninsula (AQAP), the Taliban in Pakistan and Afghanistan, Abu Sayyaf, Boko Haram and dozens of other lesser known groups - sometimes in coordination with local criminals – use a variety of funding methods. Generally speaking they keep their money within their networks and have relatively little interaction or reliance on international financial systems. That is why our financial countermeasures such as financial intelligence, sanctions, and designations are for the most part ineffective against terror groups. I explain this in my book *Hide & Seek: Intelligence, Law Enforcement and the Stalled War on Terror Finance* (2006, Potomac Books).

These groups and others like them often use cash, gold, and traditional, ethnic-based or cultural systems such as hawala and trade-based money laundering and value transfer. Although open source reporting is sketchy, these informal systems are all believed to be used in KRE.

The FATF defines TBML as "the process of disguising the proceeds of crime and moving value through the use of trade transactions in an attempt to legitimize their illicit origins."[ix] In relation to terror-finance, TBML takes a wide variety of forms. For example, it could be simple barter or a commodity-for-commodity exchange. In certain parts of Afghanistan and Pakistan, for example, the going rate for a kilo of heroin is a television set. Drug warlords exchange one commodity they control (opium) for others that they desire (luxury and sports utility vehicles). However, generally speaking, money laundering and value transfer through simple invoice fraud and manipulation are most common. The key element is the misrepresentation of the trade good to transfer value between importer and exporter. The quantity, quality, and description of the trade goods can be manipulated. The shipment of the actual goods and the accompanying documentation provide cover for "payment" or the transfer of money. The manipulation often occurs either through over-or under-valuation - depending on the objective to be achieved. To move money out of a country, participants import goods at overvalued prices or export goods at undervalued prices. To move money into a country, participants import goods at undervalued prices or export goods at overvalued prices. For the most part, all of this avoids countries' financial intelligence reporting requirements. Trade-based value transfer is found in every country around the world.

Trade-based value transfer has existed long before the advent of modern "Western" banking. In areas where our adversaries operate, trade-based value transfer is part of a way of life. It is part of their culture; a way of doing business.

In addition to customs fraud, trade-based value transfer is often used to provide "counter-valuation" or a way of balancing the books in many global underground financial systems - including some that have been used to finance terror. Trade-based value transfer is found in hawala networks, most other regional "alternative remittance systems," the massive underground Chinese fei-chien "flying money system," the misuse of the Afghan Transit Trade, Iran/Dubai commercial connections, suspect international Lebanese/Hezbollah trading syndicates, non-banked lawless regimes such those in Somalia and Libya, and many more.

The magnitude of the problem is staggering. The World Bank estimates that global remittances through official channels like banks and Western Union will reach $707 billion by 2016.[x] Unofficially, nobody knows. However, the International Monetary Fund believes, "unrecorded flows through informal channels are believed to be at least 50 percent larger than recorded flows."[xi] According to these World Bank and IMF estimates, unofficial remittances are enormous! Yet we continue to ignore trade's role in underground financial systems.

Trade and underground finance are part of the kidnap for ransom equation. For example, money and value transfer services are found throughout Iraq and Syria, including in areas where ISIS operates. These financial companies or hawaladars are trusted brokers that have established relationships throughout the region, which allow them to "transfer" funds to finance trade and pay remittances, and other financial activities. Many are family, clan, or tribe centric. They operate on trust and secrecy. These money and value transfer service (MVTS) companies do not conduct electronic funds transfers as banks do but rather communicate via email, fax, or phone with a local or foreign associate to pay or receive payment from the counterparty to a transaction. The MVTS companies then settle their business at a later date, including physical cash payments or via the conventional banking system. I believe we will also be seeing the increasing use of cyber currencies to settle accounts. However, I want to again repeat and emphasize a fact that is continually overlooked; historically and culturally, in all of the areas of the world where our terrorist adversaries operate, trade is used to balance the books or settle accounts. This is often done by the process of over-or-under invoicing sometimes called "counter-valuation." For example, that is why many hawaladars have direct or indirect ties to import/export or trading companies. Examining related trading records for invoice fraud and value transfer could be the backdoor into money/value transfer systems. Unfortunately, neither the United States nor our partners are doing this.

The FATF states that TBML is one of the three largest money laundering methodologies in the world.[xii] (Money laundering through financial institutions and bulk cash smuggling are the other two).

I would like to give you just a few examples of the magnitude of the problem.

Dr. John Zdanowicz, an academic and early pioneer in the field of TBML, examined 2013 U.S. trade data primarily obtained from the U.S. Census Bureau. By examining under-valued exports ($124,116,420,714) and over-valued imports ($94,796,135,280) Dr. Zdanowicz found that $218,912,555,994 was moved out of the United States in the form of value transfer! That figure represents 5.69% of U.S. trade. Examining over-valued exports ($68,332,594,940) and under-valued imports ($272,753,571,621), Dr. Zdanowicz calculates that $341,086,166,561 was moved into the United States! That figure represents 8.87% of U.S. trade in 2013.[xiii]

I believe the United States has one of the most robust customs enforcement arms around the world. So if almost 6 – 9 percent of our trade is tainted by customs fraud and perhaps trade-based money laundering, what does that mean for the rest of the world – particularly in areas of weak governance and high corruption like areas where our adversaries operate?

In another example, Global Financial Integrity (GFI), a Washington, D.C.-based non-profit, has done considerable work in examining trade-misinvoicing. It is a method for moving money illicitly across borders, which involves deliberately misreporting the value of a commercial transaction on an invoice and other documents submitted to customs. It is a form of trade-based money laundering. In a 2014 study, GFI found that the developing world lost $6.6 trillion in illicit financial flows from 2003 to 2012, with illicit outflows alarmingly increasing at an average rate of more than approximately 9.4 percent per year.[xiv] The number is now approaching $1 trillion a year hemorrhaging from the developing world via trade-misinvoicing alone![xv]

As noted, other forms of TBML include barter trade, capital flight, tax evasion, informal value transfer systems (such as hawala), various forms of commercial fraud and trade-misinvoicing and criminal trade-based money laundering.

I have conducted numerous investigations and written extensively about TBML. Last week, a new book that I wrote was released; *Trade-Based Money Laundering: The Next Frontier in International Money Laundering Enforcement* (Wiley). In the book, I make the argument that if one includes all its varied forms, trade-based money laundering could well be the largest money laundering methodology in the world. And, unfortunately, it is also the least understood, recognized, and enforced.

I urge the subcommittee on Terrorism, Nonproliferation, and Trade to further examine TBML. There are compelling reasons to do so. A systematic crack down on trade-fraud in the United States could possibly recover hundreds of billions of dollars a year alone in lost revenue. Perhaps more importantly, increased trade transparency will better secure the homeland and could be our most effective back door into underground finance.

In *Trade-Based Money Laundering*, I detail a number of recommendations and "steps forward."[xvi] I will briefly summarize a few of them:

1. As noted, I believe TBML could be the largest and most pervasive money laundering methodology in the world. However, we do not know for certain because the issue has never been systematically examined. This is even more surprising in the United States because annually we are possibly losing billions of dollars in lost taxes due to trade-mispricing alone. While not necessarily true for all money laundering methodologies, trade generates data. I believe it is possible for economists, statisticians, and analysts to come up with a fairly accurate estimate of the overall magnitude of global TBML and value transfer. Narrowing it down to specific problematic countries is easier still.

   I suggest this subcommittee urge the Department of Treasury's Office of Intelligence and Analysis (OIA) to at least examine U.S. related data and come up with an official estimate for the amount of TBML that impacts the U.S. A generally accepted estimate of the magnitude of TBML in all its varied forms is important for a number of reasons: a.) It will provide clarity; b). It will focus attention on the issue; c.) From an enforcement perspective, the supporting analysis should provide both excellent insight into specific areas where criminals are vulnerable and promising opportunities for targeting; and d.) A systematic crack down on TBML and customs fraud will translate into enormous revenue gain for the governments involved.

2. In the world of anti-money laundering/counter-terrorist finance (AML/CFT), the FATF makes things happen. The FATF recognizes TBML is a huge concern. There is a special FATF typology report on TBML. However, in 2012 when the current FATF recommendations were reviewed and promulgated, TBML was not specifically addressed. It is past time this is done. I suggest this subcommittee contact the U.S. Department of Treasury (which heads the U.S. FATF delegation) and urge that the U.S.

introduce a resolution calling for the misuse of trade to launder money and transfer value to be examined as a possible new FATF recommendation.

3. I agree wholeheartedly with Raymond Baker of Global Financial Integrity that, "We cannot succeed in stopping the criminals while at the same time telling multinational corporations that they can continue to mis-invoice as they choose." Abusive and fraudulent pricing techniques are used every day by thousands of multi-national corporations around the world to move money and transfer value across borders. Current AML/CFT countermeasures turn a blind eye to the use of "legitimate" actors' use of shadow financial systems, questionable financial flows, offshore havens, and assorted grey techniques used for the purposes of tax evasion, wealth preservation, and increasing profits. Yet at the same time, authorities will aggressively pursue criminal organizations' use of the same techniques to move tainted money across borders. This type of intellectual and political disingenuousness and hypocrisy contributes to our underwhelming success in effectively combating money laundering and other types of financial crimes. Global corporations must embrace legitimate trade. Legitimate actors should demand trade transparency. This means respecting customs duties, VAT assessments, currency exchange regulations, AML/CFT regulations, etc. I urge Congress to work to define illicit commercial financial flows that are facilitated via trade and then create effective and enforceable measures to curtail them. These needed reforms will also add revenue.

4. Trade transparency is the single best measure to detect trade-based money laundering and associated crimes. It is something that every government and legitimate industry and trader should welcome. Discounting the unattainable, by using modern analytic tools to exploit a variety of relevant big data sets, I believe international trade transparency is theoretically achievable or certainly possible at a factor many times over what we have today. All countries track what comes in and what goes out for security, statistical and revenue purposes. So by examining and comparing one country's targeted exports with the corresponding trading partner's record of imports it is a fairly straight forward process to spot anomalies. Some trade irregularities can be easily dismissed as numerical outliers. But sometimes anomalies can be indicative of customs fraud, tax evasion, value transfer, TBML, or perhaps even underground financial systems such as hawala that are used in kidnap for ransom.

In 2004, the United States government adopted a proposal I advanced and created the world's first trade transparency unit (TTU). It is located within Homeland Security Investigations. Per the above, the TTU uses trade data and other data to identify suspect transactions. Since that time, about a dozen other countries have established similar units and over a billion dollars of cash and assets have been seized. The creation of TTUs has

15

simultaneously overlapped with exponential advances in big data and advanced analytics. Overlaying financial intelligence, law enforcement and customs data, travel data, commercial records, etc. further increases transparency and facilitates more precise targeting. And via customs-to-customs agreements, TTUs are able to exchange specific information about suspect transactions.

As I have discussed, in addition to being an innovative countermeasure to TBML and value transfer, combatting trade-fraud is a revenue enhancer for participating governments. Frankly, it is for this reason that many countries have expressed interest in the concept.

I urge Congress to fully fund the TTU initiative so as to promote its expansion. Moreover, the concept of trade transparency should be built into the US trade agenda. For example, the new Trans-Pacific Partnership (TPP) is set to lower or eliminate tariffs on everything from imported Japanese cars to New Zealand lamb, while opening two-fifths of the global economy to easier trade in services and electronic commerce.[xvii] I don't have a position on the pros and cons of the TPP. But the volume of the increased trade will provide increasing opportunities for trade-based value transfer and money laundering. I suggest we help protect abuse by insuring that every TPP signatory country establish a TTU and share appropriate targeted trade data to spot anomalies that could be indicative of trade fraud at best and TBML at worst.

I appreciate the opportunity to appear before you today and I'm happy to answer any questions you may have.

[i] Paul Adams, "Kidnap for Ransom by Extremist Groups Extracts High Price," BBC, 12 December, 2014; available online: http://www.bbc.com/news/world-asia-30384160

[ii] David S. Cohen, "Kidnapping for Ransom: The Growing Terrorist Financing Challenge," Chatham House, October 5, 2012; available online: https://www.chathamhouse.org/sites/files/chathamhouse/public/Meetings/Meeting%20Transcripts/051012Cohen.pdf

[iii] Neil Young & Associates International (NYA International) as quoted by Dina Gusovsy, "The Multibillion Dollar Business of Ransom," CNBC, July 7, 2015; available online: http://www.cnbc.com/2015/07/06/the-multi-million-dollar-business-of-ransom-.html

[iv] "Financing of the Terrorist Organization Islamic State in Iraq and the Levant," The Financial Action Task Force (FATF), February, 2015, p. 18; available online: http://www.fatf-gafi.org/media/fatf/documents/reports/Financing-of-the-terrorist-organisation-ISIL.pdf

[v] Bureau of Consular Affairs, U.S. Department of State, as quoted by Dina Gusovsy.

[vi] David Cohen

[vii] Luke Graham, "Piracy Increases 22% in Southeast Asia," CNBC, July 9, 2012; available online: http://www.cnbc.com/2015/07/09/piracy-increases-by-22-in-southeast-asia.html

[viii] FATF

[ix] "Trade-Based Money Laundering, the FATF, Executive Summary, June 23, 2006; available online:

http://www.fatf-gafi.org/media/fatf/documents/reports/Trade%20Based%20Money%20Laundering.pdf

[x] "Developing Countries To Receive Over $410 Billion in Remittances in 2013, Says World Bank," World Bank Press Release, October 2, 2013; available online: (http://www.worldbank.org/en/news/press-release/2013/10/02/developing-countries-remittances-2013-world-bank)

[xi] Dilip Ratha, "Remittances, Funds for the Folks Back Home," International Monetary Fund; available online: (http://www.imf.org/external/pubs/ft/fandd/basics/remitt.htm)

[xii] Trade-Based Money Laundering, the Financial Action Task Force (FATF) 2006, p. Executive Summary; available online: http://www.fatf-gafi.org/publications/methodsandtrends/documents/trade-basedmoneylaundering.html

[xiii] Analysis given to the author by Dr. John Zdanowicz via June 30, 2015 email

[xiv] "New Study: Crime, Corruption, Tax Evasion Drained a Record US$991.2bn in Illicit Financial Flows from Developing Economies in 2012," Global Financial Integrity; December 15, 2014, available online: http://www.gfintegrity.org/press-release/new-study-crime-corruption-tax-evasion-drained-a-record-us991-2-billion-in-illicit-financial-flows-from-developing-economies-in-2012/

[xv] Raymond Baker, Global Financial Integrity, Seminar on "Illicit Financial Flows: The Most Damaging Economic Problem Facing the Developing World," September 21, 2015 at the National Press Club, Washington, D.C.

[xvi] John Cassara, Trade-Based Money Laundering: The Next Frontier in International Money Laundering Enforcement, Wiley, Hoboken, New Jersey, 2015; see chapter 11, pages 177 – 194.

[xvii] William Mauldin, "Details of Pacific Trade Pact Fuel Debate," Wall Street Journal, November 5, 2015; available online: http://www.wsj.com/articles/pacific-trade-agreement-terms-herald-public-battle-1446712646

Mr. POE. The Chair will recognize Dr. Weinberg for your statement.

STATEMENT OF DAVID ANDREW WEINBERG, PH.D., SENIOR FELLOW, FOUNDATION FOR DEFENSE OF DEMOCRACIES

Mr. WEINBERG. Chairman Poe, Ranking Member Keating and distinguished members of the subcommittee, thank you on behalf of the Foundation for Defense of Democracy's Center on Sanctions and Illicit Finance for the opportunity to be here today.

I will highlight some worrisome weak links in America's efforts to convince our allies to target financial facilitators and private donors to terrorism who often go unpunished.

I will also offer some policy recommendations to hopefully help address the growing epidemic of kidnapping by terrorists for ransom.

While I will defer to others on this panel regarding antiquities trafficking, I would ask your approval to enter into the record CSIF's new report by Yaya Fanusie and Alex Joffe on antiquities trafficking in financing the Islamic State.

Mr. POE. Without objection, that will be made part of the record. Thank you, Dr. Weinberg.

Mr. WEINBERG. Thank you.

Several of America's Mideast allies, namely, Qatar, Kuwait, Saudi Arabia and Turkey, unfortunately pursue problematic or even adversarial positions over tackling private terror finance.

Despite promises to do so, they have failed to effectively obstruct the flow of such funds and to try punishing its practitioners.

In my written testimony, I note dozens of reported examples of such negligence. In many instances, these governments grant legal impunity to people whom the U.S. and the U.N. have sanctioned on charges of funding al-Qaeda.

In my written remarks, I also reveal new indications that Turkey, Qatar and Saudi Arabia have let their territories become major financial hubs for Hamas.

To ensure that our Government's terror finance sanctions list isn't treated in the region as a mere toothless piece of paper, the U.S. should develop a broader range of options for when our allies refuse to do the right thing versus terror financiers.

Congress can help sensitize members of the executive branch outside of Treasury to these concerns. When the U.S. is absolutely confident that an individual who enjoys legal impunity in one of these jurisdictions is indeed a senior financial facilitator for terrorism, the U.S. could privately and then publicly seek that individual's extradition.

If that fails, the U.S. could even consider capturing and killing them as it does toward other terrorist operatives.

Congress could help hold these governments responsible as well for extending such impunity by restricting trade in dual-use items as suggested under the Export Administration Act of 1979 and by, again, amending the Foreign Sovereign Immunity Act so victims of terrorism and their families can sue foreign governments in civil court for letting terror financiers and other operatives enjoy local impunity.

As for the vicious terrorist tactic of kidnapping for ransom, we should recognize that Americans are still evidently being held hostage by terrorists today.

In 2012, Treasury described kidnapping for ransom as ''today's most significant source of terror financing.'' Now, the volume of that income has only increased since then.

ISIS actually makes more money off of oil sales, but ransoms have helped it and al-Qaeda conquer that territory in the first place. The Obama administration announced a new hostage policy in June which was mainly comprised of efforts to be more responsive and effective at hostage recovery.

But there is little sign that this is being matched by efforts to decrease the money that terrorists take in from such tactics, even though the New York Times, AP, Reuters and the Wall Street Journal have described allied governments in Europe or in the Gulf as sources of such payments.

Although these states deny paying ransoms, the Journal called such state payments game changers which can fuel the growth in ransom payments and incentivize future kidnappings.

Doha's reported role is particularly striking. In my written testimony I compiled press reports of 15 different episodes within 3 years alone in which Qatar is reported to have helped mediate hostage talks, typically with terrorists, and often in which a multi-million-dollar ransom was discussed or allegedly paid to the terrorists by Qatar.

The U.S. should stigmatize governments that pay state ransoms. Congress could require the administration to expose such governments in public, perhaps even imposing targeted financial sanctions.

President Obama should also direct diplomats to prioritize convincing those governments in several key countries to stop paying such state ransoms and Congress can encourage policy makers abroad to enact such prohibitions into local law.

The U.S. could also follow in Britain's steps, blocking insurance companies from reimbursing ransoms to terrorists, but only provided this can be done in a manner that would not impose an undue additional burden on hostages' families.

Finally, Congress and the administration could consider starting a fund with seized terrorist assets to compensate kidnapping victims and their families for their suffering.

The good news is that the U.S. now has a plan to try and improve efforts at hostage recovery and the proof will be in how well those steps are implemented.

The bad news is that U.S. policy is failing to deter foreign governments primarily our allies from paying multi-million-dollar ransoms that enrich terrorists and incentivize future attacks.

Our Government needs a new strategy to address this critical part of the problem and Congress can help facilitate that debate.

Thank you very much.

[The prepared statement of Mr. Weinberg follows:]

Terrorist Financing:

Kidnapping, Antiquities Trafficking, and Private Donations

David Andrew Weinberg, Ph.D.
Senior Fellow
Center on Sanctions and Illicit Finance
Foundation for Defense of Democracies

Hearing before the
House Committee on Foreign Affairs
Subcommittee on Terrorism, Nonproliferation, and Trade

Washington, D.C.
November 17, 2015

FDD
FOUNDATION FOR
DEFENSE OF DEMOCRACIES   1726 M Street NW • Suite 700 • Washington, DC 20036

David Andrew Weinberg   November 17, 2015

Chairman Poe, Ranking Member Keating, and distinguished Members of the Subcommittee, thank you on behalf of the Foundation for Defense of Democracies' Center on Sanctions and Illicit Finance for the chance to testify before you today.

As a think tank analyst who focuses on the Arab Gulf monarchies, I have concluded that several of America's allies in the Middle East – namely, Qatar, Turkey, Kuwait, and Saudi Arabia – are best characterized as America's frenemies on the issue of terror finance: important partners on some issues that pursue problematic or adversarial positions over terror finance emanating from their territories. As such, I will devote a significant portion of my testimony today to documenting these countries' negligence on combating private terror finance and recommending steps that Washington can take to highlight and disincentivize such harmful conduct.

However, because we are joined by Diane Foley here today, I would first like to take the opportunity to seriously grapple with the challenge posed to American interests by the problem of non-state terrorists who increasingly use kidnapping for ransom to fund their violent activities.

The toll that kidnapping takes on victims, families, employers, and their communities is immense. Perhaps because the magnitude of this toll is so difficult for the rest of us to fully comprehend, I believe that there is a tendency for policymakers to be somewhat callous or even Pollyannaish by presuming that this problem can be addressed without a serious new investment of resources and rethinking of U.S. policies in this issue area. And all this must be done without letting the heinous crimes of terrorists exert control over our decisions by forcing under- or over-reactions in American foreign policy.

I believe that the Obama administration's new policies for addressing hostage issues are a big step in the right direction that should be applauded. However, they fall short in one critical area by failing to articulate a coherent and viable new strategy to deter foreign governments, in both Europe and the Gulf, from allegedly continuing to pay direct or indirect state ransoms to terrorists on a massive scale.

I believe I witnessed a starker version of such wishful thinking as a one-time staffer on this Committee. I watched with astonishment as my boss and mentor, the late Chairman Tom Lantos (D, CA), put his arm around the wife of an Israeli soldier kidnapped by Hezbollah and inaccurately promised her that America would help bring her husband home alive. Sadly, we later learned that her husband had already passed away, having succumbed to wounds incurred when he was captured.

Rather than letting ourselves be blinded by optimism or idealism, we must recognize that U.S. policy today is failing to deter our own allies from fueling the terrorist threat by irresponsibly rewarding kidnapping for ransom at a state level.

Finally, while this hearing will also focus on the terror finance challenge of antiquities trafficking by violent groups such as the Islamic State (IS), I will defer to the other witnesses in this regard. I would also like to note that FDD's Center on Sanctions and Illicit Finance has a forthcoming comprehensive report in which coauthors Yaya Fanusie and Alex Joffe analyze the strategic role of antiquities trafficking in financing the Islamic State.

David Andrew Weinberg   November 17, 2015

Why Do Ransoms and Private Donations Matter?

While terrorist groups that now hold large swaths of territory such as the Islamic State have access to more lucrative potential sources of income – such as oil smuggling, local extortion, and bank robberies – ransoms from kidnapping as well as private terror finance from foreign donors or financial facilitators still represent an irreplaceable part of the terrorists' financial network and lifecycle.

These unique sources of income provide the critical seed funding needed for terrorist groups to establish themselves and begin to conquer that lucrative territory in the first place, as was the case for al-Qaeda's branches in North Africa and in Syria. In other cases, donations and ransoms have provided an essential lifeline to established terrorist organizations that have fallen on hard times, sustaining the Islamic State's forerunner, al-Qaeda in Iraq, after the surge and until its resurgence by exploiting Syria's civil war. Such funding sources similarly enabled al-Qaeda's branch in Yemen to recover from an American-backed counterinsurgency campaign, conquering new territory and positioning al-Qaeda for a more recent resurgence by taking advantage of Yemen's latest civil war this past year.

Donations and kidnapping for ransom play a greater role in al-Qaeda's internal finances than for the Islamic State, but they are expected to play an increasingly important role in IS's finances as well once coalition efforts to deprive it of the benefits of territory and oil smuggling begin to take effect. In addition, a senior Treasury Department official noted earlier this year that "externally raised funds" play a unique role in funding terrorist activity because they "are used frequently to finance the travel of extremists to Syria and Iraq," where tens of thousands of fighters have left their homes in over 90 countries to join up with IS or al-Qaeda.[1]

Part I. Kidnapping for Ransom
by Terrorist Groups

Kidnapping for ransom by terrorist groups is a growing problem, and one only has to consider the courageous life of Diane's son James Foley to recognize the human toll this malicious practice can exact. According to European hostages of the Islamic State who survived to tell of their experiences because ransoms were paid in their cases, Foley was singled out, even among the American hostages, for the group's worst torture. Yet even though he and the other Americans were starved for an extended period on the equivalent of just a teacup of food per day, he shared his limited rations with fellow prisoners.[2] Further, none of this could have transpired except

---

[1] U.S. Treasury Department. "Remarks of Deputy Assistant Secretary for Terrorist Financing Jennifer Fowler at the Washington Institute for Near East Policy on U.S. Efforts to Counter ISIL," February 2, 2015. (http://www.treasury.gov/press-center/press-releases/Pages/jl9755.aspx)

[2] Rukmini Callimachi. "The Horror before the Beheadings: ISIS Hostages Endured Torture and Dashed Hopes, Freed Cellmates Say." *New York Times*, October 25, 2014. (http://www.nytimes.com/2014/10/26/world/middleeast/horror-before-the-beheadings-what-isis-hostages-endured-in-syria.html?_r=0)

David Andrew Weinberg   November 17, 2015

because Foley chose to report on the Syrian people's suffering after having previously been held hostage in Libya in 2011.[3]

According to President Obama's chief counterterrorism advisor Lisa Monaco, over thirty Americans were being held hostage abroad as of June 2015.[4] Several of those individuals are still being held by state sponsors of terrorism or by non-state terror groups. For instance, the Taliban is believed to be holding hostage the American Caitlin Coleman, the baby she gave birth to in captivity, and Caitlin's husband, Canadian Joshua Boyle.[5]

In 2012, Washington's top official for combating terror finance cited kidnapping for ransom (KFR) as "today's most significant source of terrorist financing."[6] Since then, al-Qaeda and the Islamic State have conquered more territory and thus have other, larger sources of revenue, but their proceeds from KFR have only increased.[7]

Indeed, in October 2014 a report by U.N. counterterrorism officials emphasized that "the use of kidnapping for ransom as a tactic continues to grow, as does the revenue generated therefrom by groups associated with Al-Qaida."[8] The British Foreign Office similarly notes that kidnappers' demands have also increased in value.[9]

U.S. government figures compiled by Rukmini Callimachi of the *New York Times* indicate that ransoms paid to terrorist groups totaled roughly $165 million from 2008 through 2014. $125 million of that went to al-Qaeda and its direct affiliates, of which $66 million was paid in 2013 alone.[10] The Islamic State is believed to have received between $20 million and $45 million in ransoms during 2014.[11] However, the group often chooses to execute foreign hostages when a ransom is not paid or for vicious propaganda purposes instead.

---

[3] Lawrence Wright, "Five Hostages," *The New Yorker*, July 6, 2015. (http://www.newyorker.com/magazine/2015/07/06/five-hostages)

[4] Jeremy Diamond and Sunlen Serfaty, "White House Says More than 30 Americans Held Hostage Abroad," *CNN*, June 24, 2015. (http://www.cnn.com/2015/06/23/politics/hostage-policy-review-changes-white-house/)

[5] Shane Harris, "An American Mom and her Baby are being Held Hostage by the Taliban," *Daily Beast*, April 23, 2015. (http://www.thedailybeast.com/articles/2015/04/23/an-american-mom-and-her-baby-are-being-held-hostage-by-the-taliban.html)

[6] U.S. Treasury Department, "Remarks of Under Secretary David Cohen at Chatham House on the Growing Terrorist Financing Challenge," October 5, 2012. (http://www.treasury.gov/press-center/press-releases/Pages/tg1726.aspx)

[7] Jamie Dettmer, "Al Qaeda Growing Rich Off Ransom Payments," *Daily Beast*, December 22, 2012; (http://www.thedailybeast.com/articles/2013/12/22/al-qaeda-growing-rich-off-ransom-payments.html) & U.S. Treasury Department, "Remarks of Under Secretary Cohen at CSIS," June 2, 2014. (http://www.treasury.gov/press-center/press-releases/Pages/jl2415.aspx)

[8] United Nations, "Sixteenth Report of the Analytical Support and Sanctions Monitoring Team submitted pursuant to resolution 2161 (2014) concerning Al-Qaida and associated individuals and entities," September 29, 2014. (http://www.un.org/ga/search/view_doc.asp?symbol=S/2014/770)

[9] Jamie Dettmer, "Al Qaeda Growing Rich Off Ransom Payments," *Daily Beast*, December 22, 2012. (http://www.thedailybeast.com/articles/2013/12/22/al-qaeda-growing-rich-off-ransom-payments.html)

[10] Rukmini Callimachi, "Paying Ransoms, Europe Bankrolls Qaeda Terror," *New York Times*, July 29, 2014. (http://www.nytimes.com/2014/07/30/world/africa/ransoming-citizens-europe-becomes-al-qaedas-patron.html?_r=1)

[11] U.S. Treasury Department, "Remarks of Under Secretary for Terrorism and Financial Intelligence David S. Cohen at The Carnegie Endowment For International Peace, 'Attacking ISIL's Financial Foundation,'" October 23, 2014. (http://www.treasury.gov/press-center/press-releases/Pages/jl2672.aspx); Financial Action Task Force, "Financing

David Andrew Weinberg   November 17, 2015

KFR has greater importance for al-Qaeda than IS, with U.N. experts recently describing it as "the core al-Qaida tactic for generating revenue."[12] U.S. officials warned in 2014 that "ransoms have become the main source of funding for al-Qaeda-related groups in Yemen and North Africa, and an important source for such groups in Syria and Iraq."[13] According to captured al-Qaeda documents, the group's central command in Pakistan is directly involved in overseeing hostage talks as far afield as Africa.[14]

Perhaps because al-Qaeda's donors are rarely focused on causes in North Africa, the group's branch there, al-Qaeda in the Islamic Maghreb (AQIM), carved out a role as "the al-Qa'ida affiliate that has likely profited most from kidnapping for ransom."[15] The group got its start with €5 million in seed funding from a German government ransom for 32 European hostages in 2003.[16] Since 2010, AQIM has reportedly brought in between $75 million and $91.5 million from KFR alone, helping fuel its territorial expansion in northern Mali.[17]

Similarly, al-Qaeda in the Arabian Peninsula (AQAP), "used ransom money it received for the return of European hostages to finance its over $20 million campaign to seize territory in Yemen between mid-2011 and mid-2012."[18] Internal documents suggest that at one point over half of AQAP's budget was funded by KFR.[19]

of the Terrorist Organisation Islamic State in Iraq and the Levant (ISIL), February 2015, p. 20. (http://www.fatf-gafi.org/media/fatf/documents/reports/Financing-of-the-terrorist-organisation-ISIL.pdf)

[12] Edith M. Lederer, "UN: Islamic State Group Got up to $45M in Ransoms." Associated Press, November 25, 2015. (http://www.militarytimes.com/story/military/pentagon/2014/11/25/is-randoms-112414/70081514/)

[13] Ellen Knickmeyer. "Al Qaeda-Linked Groups Increasingly Funded by Ransom." Wall Street Journal, July 29. 2014. (http://www.wsj.com/articles/ransom-fills-terrorist-coffers-1406637010)

[14] "Spoils of Kidnapping are Financing al-Qaida, Reveals New York Times." PBS NewsHour, July 30, 2014. (http://www.pbs.org/newshour/bb/spoils-kidnapping-financing-al-qaida-reveals-new-york-times/)

[15] U.S. Treasury Department, "Remarks of Under Secretary David Cohen at Chatham House on the Growing Terrorist Financing Challenge." October 5, 2012. (http://www.treasury.gov/press-center/press-releases/Pages/tg1726.aspx)

[16] "Terrorgruppe Ansar al-Din: Islamistenführer in Mali war Helfer der Bundesregierung," Der Spiegel (Germany), January 20, 2013. (http://www.spiegel.de/politik/ausland/mali-islamistenfuehrer-war-helfer-der-bundesregierung-a-878572.html); Rukmini Callimachi. "Paying Ransoms, Europe Bankrolls Qaeda Terror," New York Times, July 29, 2014. (http://www.nytimes.com/2014/07/30/world/africa/ransoming-citizens-europe-becomes-al-qaedas-patron.html?_r=1)

[17] Rukmini Callimachi, "Paying Ransoms, Europe Bankrolls Qaeda Terror," New York Times, July 29, 2014. (http://www.nytimes.com/2014/07/30/world/africa/ransoming-citizens-europe-becomes-al-qaedas-patron.html?_r=1); United Nations, "Sixteenth Report of the Analytical Support and Sanctions Monitoring Team submitted pursuant to resolution 2161 (2014) concerning Al-Qaida and associated individuals and entities." September 29, 2014. (http://www.un.org/ga/search/view_doc.asp?symbol=S/2014/770); U.S. Treasury Department, "Remarks of Under Secretary for Terrorism and Financial Intelligence David Cohen before the Center for a New American Security on 'Confronting New Threats in Terrorist Financing,'" March 4, 2014. (http://www.treasury.gov/press-center/press-releases/Pages/jl2308.aspx)

[18] U.S. Treasury Department, "Remarks of Under Secretary for Terrorism and Financial Intelligence David Cohen before the Center for a New American Security on 'Confronting New Threats in Terrorist Financing,'" March 4, 2014. (http://www.treasury.gov/press-center/press-releases/Pages/jl2308.aspx)

[19] Rukmini Callimachi. "Paying Ransoms, Europe Bankrolls Qaeda Terror," New York Times, July 29, 2014. (http://www.nytimes.com/2014/07/30/world/africa/ransoming-citizens-europe-becomes-al-qaedas-patron.html?_r=1)

Other non-state terror groups that have purportedly received ransoms of $10 million or more have included the Nusra Front, al-Shabaab, FARC, and Boko Haram.[20] Terrorist organizations that have employed KFR to lesser effect include the Pakistani Taliban, Abu Sayyaf Group in the Philippines, and the Boko Haram splinter group Ansaru.[21] Palestinian terrorist groups such as Hamas and Hezbollah have also used kidnapping to extract concessions from Israel in the form of very large prisoner releases, but funding is less often a motive in such attacks.

Who Pays the Ransoms?

Unfortunately, U.S. allies in Europe and the Gulf seem to be a big part of this problem. While the American and British governments have long adhered to a policy of refusing to pay state ransoms to hostage takers, especially those involving terrorist groups, many of our allies have been far less scrupulous. As U.S. officials have warned, this creates "a genuinely vicious cycle" because "each transaction encourages another transaction" by incentivizing future kidnappings.[22] The conduct of certain American allies in this regard makes the Mideast more unstable and puts all of our citizens at greater risk.

It is important to emphasize, however, that the assertions in this testimony are not based on my own first-hand knowledge of ransoms being paid but rather based on the facts as reported by American and regional media outlets on this important but rather opaque issue. I would highly recommend following up with the allied governments described in this report as well as with the U.S. intelligence community in order to verify the reported claims that have been compiled here.

As Rukmini Callimachi concluded in her 2014 *New York Times* investigation of ransom payments to terrorists by U.S. allies, "Europe has become an inadvertent underwriter of Al Qaeda."[23] According to the *Associated Press*, "diplomats say ransoms paid or arranged by western European governments and the Gulf state of Qatar have provided the bulk of financial support for violent

---

[20] U.S. Treasury Department, "Remarks of Under Secretary Cohen at CSIS," June 2, 2014. (http://www.treasury.gov/press-center/press-releases/Pages/jl2415.aspx); Haroon Siddique, "Ransom Claim in Ingrid Betancourt Release," *The Guardian (UK)*, July 4, 2008. (http://www.theguardian.com/world/2008/jul/04/betancourt.france)

[21] U.S. Treasury Department, "Remarks of Under Secretary for Terrorism and Financial Intelligence David Cohen before the Center for a New American Security on 'Confronting New Threats in Terrorist Financing,'" March 4, 2014. (http://www.treasury.gov/press-center/press-releases/Pages/jl2308.aspx); United Nations, "Sixteenth Report of the Analytical Support and Sanctions Monitoring Team submitted pursuant to resolution 2161 (2014) concerning Al-Qaida and associated individuals and entities," September 29, 2014. (http://www.un.org/ga/search/view_doc.asp?symbol=S/2014/770); U.S. Treasury Department, "Remarks of Under Secretary David Cohen at Chatham House on the Growing Terrorist Financing Challenge," October 5, 2012. (http://www.treasury.gov/press-center/press-releases/Pages/tg1726.aspx)

[22] U.S. Treasury Department, "Remarks of Under Secretary David Cohen at Chatham House on the Growing Terrorist Financing Challenge," October 5, 2012. (http://www.treasury.gov/press-center/press-releases/Pages/tg1726.aspx)

[23] Rukmini Callimachi, "Paying Ransoms, Europe Bankrolls Qaeda Terror," *New York Times*, July 29, 2014. (http://www.nytimes.com/2014/07/30/world/africa/ransoming-citizens-europe-becomes-al-qaedas-patron.html?_r=1)

David Andrew Weinberg   November 17, 2015

groups."[24] *Reuters* reports that "Qatari officials deny paying ransom for hostages, but Western diplomatic sources in Doha say otherwise."[25]

Amidst such denials, Doha's foreign minister has evidently recognized that paying ransoms could be viewed as terror finance, noting "this is another way of fueling, if you may call it supporting through the backdoor."[26] And that is exactly what this problem has become: a pressing top concern for American officials who combat the funding of terror.

Sometimes families or corporations make the gut-wrenching decision to pay ransoms to rescue their loved ones or employees from captivity. However, it is the willingness of certain governments to pay such ransoms that has caused this problem to balloon out of control. As the *Wall Street Journal* reported last year, "diplomats and officials said" that "government-paid ransoms have been game-changers" in contributing to the recent increase in ransom payments and subsequent kidnappings.[27]

Europe:

Until America's European allies join us and Britain by stopping the direct or indirect flow of multimillion dollar ransoms to terrorist organizations, perhaps it makes more sense to speak of them as *incontinental* Europe to stigmatize their undisciplined behavior.

Despite being obligated under new G8, OSCE, and U.N. Security Council rules not to do so, some European governments reportedly continue to pay ransoms. Earlier this year, a top Treasury official confirmed in a public speech that despite these highly visible commitments, "certain countries have adopted a de facto policy of allowing the payment of ransoms on a case-by-case basis... particularly in Europe and the Middle East."[28]

Most notably, Washington and London elicited a G8 statement in June 2013 that "we unequivocally reject the payment of ransoms to terrorists."[29] Jamie Dettmer of the *Daily Beast* writes that "the leaders of France, Italy, Canada and Germany all endorsed the no-ransom agreement but all those countries have paid out ransoms for their kidnapped citizens or provided tacit approval for payments made by businesses and NGOs — perhaps since the G8 summit — say

---

[24] Lara Jakes and Ellen Knickmeyer, "Foley Case Lays Bare Debate over Paying Ransom," *Associated Press*, August 21. 2014. (http://bigstory.ap.org/article/official-militants-asked-1325-million-ransom)

[25] Amena Bakr, "Qatar Pares Support for Islamists but Careful to Preserve Ties," *Reuters*, November 2, 2014. (http://www.reuters.com/article/2014/11/02/us-mideast-crisis-qatar-insight-idUSKBN0IM07B20141102)

[26] Peter Kovessy, "Foreign Minister: Qatar Does Not Pay Ransoms," *Doha News*, September 30. 2014. (http://dohanews.co/foreign-minister-qatar-pay-ransoms/)

[27] Ellen Knickmeyer, "Al Qaeda-Linked Groups Increasingly Funded by Ransom," *Wall Street Journal*, July 29, 2014. (http://www.wsj.com/articles/ransom-fills-terrorist-coffers-1406637010)

[28] U.S. Treasury Department, "Remarks of Deputy Assistant Secretary for Terrorist Financing Jennifer Fowler at the Washington Institute for Near East Policy on U.S. Efforts to Counter ISIL," February 2, 2015. (http://www.treasury.gov/press-center/press-releases/Pages/jl9755.aspx)

[29] "2013 Lough Erne G8 Leaders' Communiqué," *U.K. Government online portal*, June 18, 2013. (https://www.gov.uk/government/uploads/system/uploads/attachment_data/file/207771/Lough_Erne_2013_G8_Leaders_Communique.pdf)

diplomats and security industry insiders."[30] Further, the *Times*'s Callimachi reports that "according to hostages released this year and veteran negotiators, governments in Europe — especially France, Spain and Switzerland — continue to be responsible for some of the largest payments, including a ransom of €30 million — about $40 million — paid last fall to free four Frenchmen held in Mali."[31]

Callimachi also interviewed an adviser to the president of Burkina Faso who was involved in several hostage negotiations between Europe and al-Qaeda. He indicated that he "routinely dealt with aggressive Western diplomats who demanded the release of Qaeda fighters held in local prisons in an effort to win the release of hostages," noting that "you would not believe the pressure that the West brings to bear on African countries."[32]

Callimachi's investigation also found that France was the worst long-term offender among European countries, having paid an estimated $58.1 million in ransoms to al-Qaeda or IS, followed by Switzerland and Spain in the low teens.[33] Other reports claimed that two Italian aid workers were released by the Nusra Front early last year in exchange for $12 million, although it has also been suggested that Qatar was involved in paying this specific ransom.[34] The *Economist* reported that in 2014, IS brought in "at least $20m last year from ransoms paid for hostages, including several French and Spanish journalists."[35] Although press reports alleging ransoms in these cases were dismissed by the French and Italian governments, those reports were subsequently bolstered by being publicly highlighted by top Treasury Department officials.[36]

In 2009, several European hostages were kidnapped when returning to Niger from a music festival in Mali. Two were from Switzerland, one from Germany, and one from the United Kingdom. Britain wouldn't pay a ransom to their al-Qaeda captors, and its citizen was executed while the others were released.[37] The *New York Times* quoted a European official indicating that Swiss lawmakers "voted on a national budget that 'suddenly had an extra line for humanitarian aid for Mali'" that year to be used in practice for ransom.[38]

---

[30] Jamie Dettmer, "Al Qaeda Growing Rich Off Ransom Payments," *Daily Beast*, December 22, 2012. (http://www.thedailybeast.com/articles/2013/12/22/al-qaeda-growing-rich-off-ransom-payments.html)
[31] Rukmini Callimachi, "Paying Ransoms, Europe Bankrolls Qaeda Terror," *New York Times*, July 29, 2014. (http://www.nytimes.com/2014/07/30/world/africa/ransoming-citizens-europe-becomes-al-qaedas-patron.html?_r=1)
[32] Rukmini Callimachi, "Paying Ransoms, Europe Bankrolls Qaeda Terror," *New York Times*, July 29, 2014. (http://www.nytimes.com/2014/07/30/world/africa/ransoming-citizens-europe-becomes-al-qaedas-patron.html?_r=1)
[33] Rukmini Callimachi, "Paying Ransoms, Europe Bankrolls Qaeda Terror," *New York Times*, July 29, 2014. (http://www.nytimes.com/2014/07/30/world/africa/ransoming-citizens-europe-becomes-al-qaedas-patron.html?_r=1)
[34] Stephanie Kirchgaessner, "Two Italian Aid Workers Freed in Syria after Multi-Million Dollar Ransom Paid," *The Guardian (UK)*, January 15, 2015. (http://www.theguardian.com/world/2015/jan/15/two-italian-aid-workers-freed-syria); "Syria Conflict: Italian Aid Worker Hostages Freed," *BBC*, January 16, 2015. (http://www.bbc.com/news/world-europe-30838375)
[35] "Where Islamic State Gets its Money," *The Economist (UK)*, January 4, 2015. (http://www.economist.com/blogs/economist-explains/2015/01/economist-explains)
[36] U.S. Treasury Department, "Remarks of Under Secretary for Terrorism and Financial Intelligence David S. Cohen at The Carnegie Endowment For International Peace, 'Attacking ISIL's Financial Foundation,'" October 23, 2014. (http://www.treasury.gov/press-center/press-releases/Pages/jl2672.aspx)
[37] Jamie Dettmer, "Al Qaeda Growing Rich Off Ransom Payments," *Daily Beast*, December 22, 2012. (http://www.thedailybeast.com/articles/2013/12/22/al-qaeda-growing-rich-off-ransom-payments.html)
[38] Rukmini Callimachi, "Paying Ransoms, Europe Bankrolls Qaeda Terror," *New York Times*, July 29, 2014. (http://www.nytimes.com/2014/07/30/world/africa/ransoming-citizens-europe-becomes-al-qaedas-patron.html?_r=1)

David Andrew Weinberg   November 17, 2015

Qatar:

There is one state that routinely emerges as a participant in these negotiations even though its citizens are generally not in the line of fire: the tiny Gulf nation of Qatar. And while Doha's freelancing has often proven a boon to hostages and their families in up to fifteen cases that I have identified since 2012 or 2013, its alleged role paying enormous ransoms in many of these instances should raise deep concerns for American policy in the fight against terror. Indeed, press reports suggest Doha has repeatedly been a source of multi-million dollar payments (perhaps even in the eight- or nine-figure range) that could significantly strengthen the hands of terrorists.

In Yemen, a $20.4 million ransom from Qatar and Oman went to al-Qaeda in the Arabian Peninsula on behalf of several European countries to free four hostages in 2012 and 2013, according to Yemeni and European officials.[39] Along with a 2011 ransom payment that a Western official told the *Los Angeles Times* was paid by the government of France, these funds reportedly helped AQAP recover from severe financial difficulties and played a major part in its $20+ million offensive to conquer and hold territory in several of Yemen's southern provinces.[40]

Yemen's foreign minister at the time made a rare public complaint against Qatar, warning that "these arrangements made by Qatar… may have led to a disaster," reiterating that "Yemen constantly rejects the handling of the release of kidnapped hostages through the payment of ransoms."[41] According to a senior Yemeni parliamentarian at the time, AQAP was "having crazy money problems before the kidnap ransoms. They were having to sell their guns."[42] Yemeni officials claimed they saw Qatari officials arrive on a private jet with bags they believed were filled

---

[39] Rukmini Callimachi, "Paying Ransoms, Europe Bankrolls Qaeda Terror," *New York Times*, July 29, 2014. (http://www.nytimes.com/2014/07/30/world/africa/ransoming-citizens-europe-becomes-al-qaedas-patron.html?_r=1); "Yemen Kidnappers Free Finnish Couple, Austrian," *Reuters*, May 9, 2013. (http://www.reuters.com/article/2013/05/09/us-yemen-hostages-idUSBRE9480TM20130509#vT5ieeBDKucP5ZCr.97) It is worth noting that Oman has also reportedly facilitated several releases of Americans held by Iran, the biggest state sponsor of terrorism, allegedly in a *quid pro quo* for Iranian criminals behind U.S. bars and Omani payments of hundreds of thousands of dollars; however, unlike Qatar, Oman's involvement in alleged ransom payments to al-Qaeda seems to be limited to this single Yemeni case: Jay Solomon, "Secret Dealings with Iran Led to Nuclear Talks: Years of Clandestine Exchanges between the Two Countries Helped Build a Foundation for Nuclear Negotiations," *Wall Street Journal*, June 28, 2015. (http://www.wsj.com/articles/iran-wish-list-led-to-u-s-talks-1435537004?alg=y) A source close to Yemeni President Abd Rabbuh Mansour Hadi also allegedly indicated that the UAE paid a ransom to AQAP in order to free British hostage Douglas Semple instead of freeing him in a military operation this past August as publicly claimed: Rori Donaghy, "UAE Paid Ransom to Yemeni Tribesmen to Free British Hostage," *Middle East Eye (UK)*, August 27, 2015. (http://www.middleeasteye.net/news/uae-paid-ransom-yemeni-tribesmen-free-british-hostage-1676587015)
[40] Ken Dilanian, "Al Qaeda Group is Operating on Ransom Money from the West," *Los Angeles Times*, October 21, 2013. (http://articles.latimes.com/2013/oct/21/world/la-fg-yemen-ransom-20131021); Rukmini Callimachi, "Yemen Terror Boss Left Blueprint for Waging Jihad," *Associated Press*, August 9, 2013. (http://www.ap.org/Content/AP-In-The-News/2013/Yemen-terror-boss-left-blueprint-for-waging-jihad); U.S. Treasury Department, "Remarks of Under Secretary for Terrorism and Financial Intelligence David Cohen before the Center for a New American Security on 'Confronting New Threats in Terrorist Financing,'" March 4, 2014. (http://www.treasury.gov/press-center/press-releases/Pages/jl2308.aspx)
[41] Ellen Knickmeyer, "Al Qaeda-Linked Groups Increasingly Funded by Ransom," *Wall Street Journal*, July 29, 2014. (http://www.wsj.com/articles/ransom-fills-terrorist-coffers-1406637010)
[42] Ellen Knickmeyer, "Al Qaeda-Linked Groups Increasingly Funded by Ransom," *Wall Street Journal*, July 29, 2014. (http://www.wsj.com/articles/ransom-fills-terrorist-coffers-1406637010)

David Andrew Weinberg   November 17, 2015

with cash; the jet then carried back a Swiss hostage from al-Qaeda to Qatar, where she was received by the Swiss ambassador to Doha.[43]

But it's in Syria and Iraq where the Qatari role as a hostage mediator has really come to the fore in the last few years.

In October 2013, *McClatchy's* Mitchell Prothero reported that Qatar's foreign minister "personally negotiated [a] deal with Syrian rebels" to release nine Shi'ite Lebanese pilgrims captured near Aleppo to coincide with the release of two Turkish Airlines pilots who had been separately kidnapped in Lebanon.[44] Prothero noted that "local media reports claimed that Qatar had paid as much as $150 million to secure the release of the hostages." He noted that *McClatchy* spoke to a Lebanese security official who stated that "the $150 million figure seemed high" but "that the deal did include money paid by Qatar."[45] Columnist Yusuf Kanlı of the Turkish daily *Hürriyet* also noted the alleged figure of $150 million, stating that the "ransom is said to have been paid to the Sunni al-Nusra group (an al-Qaeda branch)" and that the Turkish pilots were delivered from Lebanon to Turkey on a jet from Qatar's national carrier, Qatar Airways.[46] The Lebanese paper *al-Liwa* reported that Qatar paid the rebels €100 million, citing a Turkish source in Istanbul and claiming that the amount was confirmed by the Syrian Observatory for Human Rights; the paper claimed that the Syrian regime released over 100 prisoners as part of the trade and showed a picture of the pilgrims purportedly returning home on a plane from Qatar Airways' charter flights subsidiary, Qatar Executive.[47]

In March 2014, Qatari and Lebanese mediation helped free thirteen Syrian nuns and three other women being held hostage by the Nusra Front. According to Ellen Knickmeyer of the *Wall Street Journal*, "Qatar paid a $16 million ransom, according to a Lebanese official."[48] Journalist Robert Fisk reported that other Lebanese sources put the ransom as high as £40 million and that Syrian sources put the amount at £43 million, although the nuns themselves claimed no ransom was paid at all.[49] Other sources claim that Qatar offered to pay $4 million for the nuns[50] and that the

[43] Ellen Knickmeyer, "Al Qaeda-Linked Groups Increasingly Funded by Ransom," *Wall Street Journal*, July 29, 2014. (http://www.wsj.com/articles/ransom-fills-terrorist-coffers-1406637010)
[44] Mitchell Prothero, "Lebanese Pilgrims Held for Year by Syrian Rebels back in Beirut," *McClatchy*, October 19, 2013. (http://www.mcclatchydc.com/news/nation-world/world/middle-east/article24757552.html)
[45] Mitchell Prothero, "Lebanese Pilgrims Held for Year by Syrian Rebels back in Beirut," *McClatchy*, October 19, 2013. (http://www.mcclatchydc.com/news/nation-world/world/middle-east/article24757552.html)
[46] Yusuf Kanlı, "Is Turkish Foreign Policy Successful?" *Hürriyet Daily News (Turkey)*, October 21, 2013. (http://www.hurriyetdailynews.com/is-turkish-foreign-policy-successful.aspx?pageID=449&nID=56527&NewsCatID=425)
[47] "قطر تدفع ١٥٠ مليون دولار لتحرير مخطوفي أعزاز" *al-Liwa (Lebanon)*, October 19, 2013. (http://www.aliwaa.com/Article.aspx?ArticleId=182358); "الذكرى الأولى لإستشهاد الحسن" *al-Liwa (Lebanon)*. October 21, 2013. (http://www.aliwaa.com/Article.aspx?ArticleId=182474)
[48] Ellen Knickmeyer, "Al Qaeda-Linked Groups Increasingly Funded by Ransom," *Wall Street Journal*, July 29, 2014. (http://www.wsj.com/articles/ransom-fills-terrorist-coffers-1406637010); "صحيفة لبنانية: قطر سددت 16 مليون دولار" "إتمام صفقة راهبات معلولا" *Youm al-Sabi (Egypt)*, March 10, 2014. (http://goo.gl/ji8sTo)
[49] Robert Fisk, "Qatar Paid Syrian rebels £40m ransom to free nuns - or did it?" *Belfast Telegraph (Ireland)*, March 19, 2014. (http://www.belfasttelegraph.co.uk/news/world-news/qatar-paid-syrian-rebels-40m-ransom-to-free-nuns-or-did-it-30104907.html)
[50] Anne Barnard and Hwaida Saad. "Nuns Released by Syrians after Three-Month Ordeal," *New York Times*. March 9, 2014. (http://www.nytimes.com/2014/03/10/world/middleeast/nuns-released-by-syrians-after-three-month-ordeal.html)

David Andrew Weinberg   November 17, 2015

kidnappers ultimately did receive $4 million plus the release of over 150 prisoners from Syrian jail.[51]

In August 2014, Qatar's mediation helped secure the release of U.S. hostage Theo Padnos (aka Peter Theo Curtis) from the grips of al-Qaeda's Nusra Front in Syria. Shane Harris and James Kirchick of the *Daily Beast* reported that "sources close to efforts to free other Americans held abroad said that Qatar facilitated a ransom payment to help free journalist Peter Theo Curtis."[52] Harris later elaborated as follows: "Two sources familiar with efforts to free Curtis told The Daily Beast that Qatar arranged for money to be paid to the al Qaeda branch—effectively a ransom. A third source, who is a former U.S. law enforcement official, denied that the money was a direct ransom payment, but said that Qatari officials had helped negotiate with al Qaeda in Syria to win Curtis's release. What the militants may have received in return, this person declined to say."[53] Ransom demands in Padnos's case reportedly started at $3 million and went up to $25 million.[54]

In September 2014, Qatar mediated between the Nusra Front and the Fijian government for the release of 45 Fijian peacekeepers taken while serving as part of the U.N. force stationed between Syria and the Israeli-controlled Golan Heights. According to the pan-Arab paper *Asharq al-Awsat*, Syrian opposition sources told the paper that "Qatar paid in exchange a financial ransom amounting to $20 million," while pointing out "other information" claiming Qatar paid even higher, namely $1 million for each one of the 45 kidnapped soldiers.[55] Israeli TV's Channel Two aired footage it claimed showed a mediator's meeting on the Syrian side of the border with al-Qaeda's Nusra Front where a $25 million Qatari ransom for the peacekeepers was electronically deposited and confirmed in the group's bank accounts.[56]

In addition to these five cases of an alleged Qatari ransom to terrorists, I have identified up to ten other hostage cases in which Qatar purportedly also played some role, often by mediating with terrorists or in which a ransom was thought to be paid or discussed.

---

[51] "$4 million Ransom Paid for Nuns' Release." *Now Lebanon (Lebanon)*. March 10, 2014.
(https://now.mmedia.me/lb/en/inthepress/538565-4-million-ransom-paid-for-nuns-release) & see also " بوادر تقارب بين
لا معلو راهبات إطلاق بعد والنوحة دمشق" *Asharq al-Awsat (UK)*, March 11, 2014.
(http://archive.aawsat.com/details.asp?section=1&issueno=12887&article=764255#.VkIn17dJbIU)
[52] Shane Harris and James Kirchick, "Exclusive: Freed Al Qaeda Agent Was Part of Proposed Swap for Jailed Americans," *Daily Beast*, January 25, 2015. (http://www.thedailybeast.com/articles/2015/01/25/exclusive-freed-al-qaeda-agent-was-part-of-proposed-swap-for-jailed-americans.html)
[53] Shane Harris, "U.S. Pays Off Hostage Takers," *Daily Beast*, April 29, 2015.
(http://www.thedailybeast.com/articles/2015/04/29/exposed-the-white-house-s-double-game-on-hostages.html);
Lawrence Wright, "Five Hostages," *The New Yorker*, July 6, 2015.
(http://www.newyorker.com/magazine/2015/07/06/five-hostages)
[54] Rukmini Callimachi, "U.S. Writer Held by Qaeda Affiliate in Syria is Freed after Nearly 2 Years," *New York Times*, August 24, 2014. (http://www.nytimes.com/2014/08/25/world/middleeast/peter-theo-curtis-held-by-qaeda-affiliate-in-syria-is-freed-after-2-years.html?_r=0)
[55] النصرة جبهة لدى أندوف جنود عن الإفراج وساطة توليها رسميا تعلن قطر" *Asharq al-Awsat (UK)*, September 12, 2014. (http://aawsat.com/home/article/180471)
[56] "Report: UN Had Qatar Pay Off Al-Qaida Fighters for Release of Fiji Peacekeepers." *Ha'aretz (Israel)*, October 11, 2014; (http://www.haaretz.com/middle-east-news/1.620228) & "בלעדי תיעוד .מ"או הטופי עבור כופר :המצלמה לעין"
Mako (Israel), October 10, 2014. (http://www.mako.co.il/news-world/arab-q4_2014/Article-c4f048e4dd9f841004.htm?sCh=3d385dd2dd5d4110&pId=1434139730)

David Andrew Weinberg   November 17, 2015

In January 2013, Qatar and Turkey reportedly negotiated the release of 48 Iranian pilgrims from Syrian rebels in exchange for over 2,000 prisoners from Syrian jail.[57]

Qatar's role in the Obama administration's negotiations to swap Sgt. Bowe Bergdahl in May 2014 for five senior Taliban commanders is well known, and President Obama spoke with both Qatar's Emir and Father Emir in the week before Bergdahl's release.[58] What is not so well known is that "a private $10 million cash ransom deal was in the works" through other channels before that swap was implemented, according to *BuzzFeed News'* Aram Roston, although it may not have involved the Qatari or American governments. Roston also reported that the Taliban previously demanded $25 million and $15 million ransoms earlier in the process, along with the request for a much larger prisoner release involving fifty individuals.[59]

Rep. Duncan Hunter (R, CA) wrote a letter to the Pentagon later that year raising concerns that some money in Bergdahl's case may still have been disbursed: "I recognize the reluctance to describe a payment as ransom, but regardless of how the transaction is described, it has been brought to my attention that a payment was made by an Afghan intermediary who 'disappeared' with the money and failed to facilitate Bergdahl's release," adding that "the payment was made in January-February 2014, according to sources, through Joint Special Operations Command."[60]

After Theo Padnos's August 2014 release, a Qatar-based reporter wrote that a Gulf source said Qatar was trying to free four other Americans being held hostage in Syria.[61] Since James Foley had just been murdered by the Islamic State, this likely referred to the three other Americans later executed by IS – Steven Sotloff, Peter Kassig, and Kayla Mueller – plus at least one other American hostage.[62] It has also been alleged that Doha received a ransom demand for Foley before his murder, but that "the amount was huge and Qatar said no."[63]

In September 2014, Qatar's foreign minister reportedly told a Lebanese delegation visiting Doha that he had tried negotiating with the Nusra Front for the release of two Orthodox bishops in Syria but that talks fell apart when the hostages were transferred to control of the Islamic State, with which Qatar has less influence.[64] The next month, when Nusra freed a Catholic priest it had

[57] "Syrian rebels free Iranian hostages in swap," *Al Jazeera English (Qatar)*, January 9, 2013. (http://www.aljazeera.com/news/middleeast/2013/01/201319102949949456.html)

[58] Steve Holland and Warren Strobel, "Inside the White House's Decision to Free Bergdahl," *Reuters*, June 4, 2014. (http://www.reuters.com/article/2014/06/05/us-usa-bergdahl-obama-insight-idUSKBN0EG04720140605#1D2gSdLwmSo05I5v.97)

[59] Aram Roston, "Exclusive: Inside The Other Bergdahl Negotiations," *BuzzFeed News*, June 26, 2014. (http://www.buzzfeed.com/aramroston/exclusive-inside-other-bergdahl-negotiation#.jcOZ090AK)

[60] Rep. Duncan Hunter, "Letter to The Honorable Chuck Hagel," November 5, 2014. (http://online.wsj.com/public/resources/documents/2014HunterLetterNov5.pdf)

[61] Amena Bakr, "Qatar Seeks to Free More U.S. Hostages in Syria: Source," *Reuters*, August 27, 2014. (http://www.reuters.com/article/2014/08/28/us-syria-crisis-qatar-usa-idUSKBN0GQ0JW20140828#hXXhgSuO47tt7Rkd.97)

[62] See also Lawrence Wright, "Five Hostages," *The New Yorker*, July 6, 2015. (http://www.newyorker.com/magazine/2015/07/06/five-hostages)

[63] "Difficult to Find Relationship between Qatar and IS," *Deutsche Welle (Germany)*, September 3, 2014. (http://www.dw.com/en/difficult-to-find-relationship-between-qatar-and-is/a-17897307)

[64] Jean Aziz, "Qatar Foreign Minister Believes Abducted Bishops Still Alive," *Al-Monitor*, September 8, 2014. (http://www.al-monitor.com/pulse/originals/2014/09/bishop-abducted-syria-alive-qatar-mediation.html#)

David Andrew Weinberg   November 17, 2015

kidnapped several days before, the *New York Times*'s Rukmini Callimachi openly wondered "if Qatari 'mediation' was involved."[65]

At the end of 2014, Qatar found innocent and finally released two American citizens, Grace and Matthew Huang, whose prior conviction in a Qatari court for the tragic death of their adopted daughter was allegedly based on forged evidence and the racist presumption that an Asian-American couple would most likely adopt a child from Africa in order to harvest her organs.[66] Citing "two individuals with direct knowledge of the case," Harris and Kirchick of the *Daily Beast* reported that a "proposal was floated in July 2014 to the then-U.S. ambassador in Qatar by an individual acting on behalf of that country's attorney general" that the Huangs be released in exchange for Ali Saleh Kahlah al-Marri, a Qatari-Saudi dual national who was being held in federal prison after admitting in a plea deal to having been an al-Qaeda sleeper agent.[67]

As part of his U.S. plea bargain, al-Marri stated that he had been dispatched to "enter the United States no later than September 10, 2001" by Khalid Sheikh Mohammed, the mastermind of al-Qaeda's 9/11 attacks; yet he was publicly received by many Qatari elites as a returning hero[68] after being released early from federal prison in January 2015, supposedly for good behavior.[69] Rep. Duncan Hunter raised concerns after Marri's release that it indeed may have been as part of an effort to release U.S. prisoners either in Qatar or in Qatari-mediated talks with terrorists.[70]

In January 2015, Arabic news sites claimed that Italian aid workers Vanessa Marzullo and Greta Ramelli were released by the Nusra Front in return for a $12 million ransom.[71] Britain's *The Guardian* spoke to "security sources" who confirmed that a multimillion dollar ransom was paid

[65] @RCallimachi, "Franciscan priest Hanna Jallouf has been released by Nusra Front, acc. to El Mundo -- wonder if Qatari "mediation" was involved" *Twitter*, October 9, 2014.
(https://twitter.com/rcallimachi/status/520261697945489408)

[66] Rick Gladstone, "Exonerated by Qatar, American Couple Head Home," *Los Angeles Times*, December 3, 2014. (http://www.nytimes.com/2014/12/04/world/middleeast/qatar-matthew-grace-huang-return-home.html); "The U.S. Government Could Have Done a Lot More," *CBS News*, December 8, 2014.
(http://www.cbsnews.com/news/matthew-grace-huang-home-cleared-in-death-of-daughter-in-qatar/)

[67] Shane Harris and James Kirchick, "Exclusive: Freed Al Qaeda Agent Was Part of Proposed Swap for Jailed Americans," *Daily Beast*, January 25, 2015. (http://www.thedailybeast.com/articles/2015/01/25/exclusive-freed-al-qaeda-agent-was-part-of-proposed-swap-for-jailed-americans.html)

[68] David Andrew Weinberg, "Analysis: Qatar Embraces Admitted al Qaeda Operative," *Long War Journal*, January 23, 2015. (http://www.longwarjournal.org/archives/2015/01/celebrating_terror_q.php)

[69] Shane Harris and James Kirchick, "Exclusive: Freed Al Qaeda Agent Was Part of Proposed Swap for Jailed Americans," *Daily Beast*, January 25, 2015. (http://www.thedailybeast.com/articles/2015/01/25/exclusive-freed-al-qaeda-agent-was-part-of-proposed-swap-for-jailed-americans.html)

[70] Greg Richter, "Duncan Hunter: al-Qaida Operative Likely Released to Free Hostages," *Newsmax*, January 21, 2015. (http://www.newsmax.com/Newsfront/terrorist-al-marri-released-al-Qaida/2015/01/21/id/619952/); Shane Harris and James Kirchick, "Exclusive: Freed Al Qaeda Agent Was Part of Proposed Swap for Jailed Americans," *Daily Beast*, January 25, 2015. (http://www.thedailybeast.com/articles/2015/01/25/exclusive-freed-al-qaeda-agent-was-part-of-proposed-swap-for-jailed-americans.html)

[71] "دولار مليون 12 مقابل الإيطاليتين الأسيرتين عن تفرج النصرة" *al-Rai al-Aam (Kuwait)*, January 15, 2015; (http://old.alrayalaam.com/news/details/40120/?title=) & @akhbar, "عن تفرج النصرة_جبهة# : الآن_أخبار# لـمصدر" "حلب#سوريا#. دولار مليون 12 مقابل "مارزولو فانيسا" و "راميللي جريتا" الإيطاليتين الأسيرتين *Twitter*, January 15, 2015. (https://twitter.com/akhbar/status/555778189130498048)

to the Nusra Front for the two Italians,[72] and the *BBC* reported that "the BBC's Gillian Hazel in Rome says there are unconfirmed rumours that a ransom worth up to $15m (£9.9m) had been paid for the pair's release following negotiations facilitated by Qatar."[73] The Qatari-owned outlet *Al Jazeera English* broadcast what it claimed were photographs of $11 million handed over to representatives of the Nusra Front for the two women, though it suggested that really Italy was responsible for the payments.[74]

In February 2015, Indian PM Narendra Modi broke the news that a Jesuit priest from India named Father Alexis Prem Kumar had been freed after eight months in Taliban captivity. The New Delhi-based *Hindustan Times* reported that talks for his release were mediated by Qatar, took place in Doha, and were predicted on a ransom being paid, according to what Kumar's brother said the priest was told by his captors.[75] One month later, Qatar's Emir Tamim undertook his first state visit to India, where Modi sought to enlist the emir's assistance rescuing thirty-nine Indian hostages seized in Mosul by IS.[76]

In March 2015, Czech tourists Hana Humpalova and Antonie Chrastecka were released in Afghanistan after having been kidnapped two years earlier in Pakistan. The Turkish Islamist charity IHH, which assisted in their release, said that the two women had been kidnapped by gunmen from a group linked to al-Qaeda.[77] According to the Czech press, Qatar reportedly played a significant behind-the-scenes role and a ransom of $2 million was discussed after the kidnappers initially demanded $20 million for the women.[78]

A Taliban source claimed to the *Daily Beast* that until March of this year the American government was "seeking Taliban intervention to help get back U.S. hostages" in Afghanistan and Pakistan. According to Shane Harris, "the Taliban source claimed that U.S. officials told the Taliban and the government of Qatar that they'd be grateful for 'any help' bringing American hostages home."[79]

[72] Stephanie Kirchgaessner, "Two Italian Aid Workers Freed in Syria after Multi-Million Dollar Ransom Paid," *The Guardian (UK)*, January 15, 2015. (http://www.theguardian.com/world/2015/jan/15/two-italian-aid-workers-freed-syria)
[73] "Syria Conflict: Italian Aid Worker Hostages Freed," *BBC*, January 16, 2015. (http://www.bbc.com/news/world-europe-30838375)
[74] "Exclusive: Italy paying ransoms in Syria and Somalia," *Al Jazeera English (Qatar)*, October 9, 2015. (http://www.aljazeera.com/news/2015/10/exclusive-italy-paying-ransoms-syria-somalia-151007093239241.html)
[75] Harinder Baweja, "Was Taliban Paid Ransom to Release Aid Worker Alexis Prem Kumar?" *Hindustan Times*, March 5, 2015. (http://www.hindustantimes.com/india/was-taliban-paid-ransom-to-release-aid-worker-alexis-prem-kumar/story-UJJ4ym8UEPRaa7fDOo0eNK.html)
[76] "Modi Seeks Qatar's Aid in Rescuing 39 Indians Held Hostage by IS," *Press Trust of India (PTI)*, March 25, 2015. (http://www.rediff.com/news/report/modi-seeks-qatars-aid-in-rescuing-39-indians-held-hostage-by-is/20150325.htm)
[77] "2 Czech Tourists Abducted in 2013 have been Freed in Pakistan," *Associated Press*, March 28, 2015. (http://www.nytimes.com/2015/03/29/world/asia/2-czech-tourists-abducted-in-2013-have-been-freed-in-pakistan.html)
[78] "Czech Women Kidnapped in Pakistan Freed," *Czech News Agency (Czech Republic)*, March 28, 2015. (http://www.praguepost.com/the-big-story/46328-czech-women-kidnapped-in-pakistan-freed); "Qatar Assisted in Release of Two Czech Women," *Czech News Agency (Czech Republic)*, March 20, 2015. (http://www.praguepost.com/czech-news/46373-qatar-assisted-in-release-of-two-czech-women)
[79] Shane Harris, "An American Mom and her Baby are being Held Hostage by the Taliban," *Daily Beast*, April 23, 2015. (http://www.thedailybeast.com/articles/2015/04/23/an-american-mom-and-her-baby-are-being-held-hostage-by-the-taliban.html)

David Andrew Weinberg   November 17, 2015

This would presumably would have included efforts to free the Taliban's American hostage Caitlin Coleman, the baby she gave birth to in captivity, and her Canadian husband Joshua Boyle, especially since Sgt. Bergdahl had already been released in 2014 and Maryland native Warren Weinstein had been erroneously killed in a drone strike against his al-Qaeda captors in the Afghanistan-Pakistan border region that January.

Finally, Qatari mediation has played a central role negotiating directly with the Nusra Front and the Islamic State on behalf of Beirut, which seeks to free dozens of its soldiers and police officers who were captured when Syrian jihadists overran the Lebanese frontier town of Arsal.[80] Those kidnappings took place in August 2014 as part of what Lebanon's defense minister called a premeditated attack.[81] This attack on Arsal came shortly after Beirut disrupted a suspected plot to break high-value terrorist operatives out of Lebanon's Roumieh prison and after a top Nusra leader had promised those prisoners "imminent relief within days."[82]

Although the release of the Roumieh prisoners initially topped the Nusra Front's list of demands, Qatari- and Saudi-owned outlets reported that the terror group agreed this summer to a formula with "Arab and regional countries" whereby it would release the hostages for five female prisoners and $30 million in ransom from "some regional states;" however, the deal was allegedly blocked on Lebanon's side by Hezbollah.[83]

At least one of the terrorist operatives that Nusra has been trying to free from Roumieh is an individual under U.S. and U.N. terror finance sanctions who has held a Qatari ID card, goes by the nickname Umar al-Qatari, and allegedly was arrested carrying funds intended for al-Qaeda from a Qatari sheikh closely linked to the country's ruling elite.[84]

Qatar allegedly seeks to shift responsibility for its role in these cases onto Europe, insisting "don't blame us, blame the EU."[85] But while European nations only get involved when their own citizens are held captive, Qatar's motivation is far harder to justify. Its officials studiously deny the payment of ransoms in such cases and prefer to characterize their involvement as a humanitarian

[80] Thomas El-Basha, "ISIS 'Meets' Qatari Mission over Lebanon Hostages," *Al-Arabiya (UAE)*, September 7, 2014. (http://english.alarabiya.net/en/News/middle-east/2014/09/07/ISIS-meets-Qatari-mission-over-Lebanon-hostages-.html); Esperance Ghanem, "When Will Lebanon Get Their Kidnapped Soldiers Back?" *Al-Monitor.* October 16, 2015. (http://www.al-monitor.com/pulse/originals/2015/10/lebanon-kidnapped-soldiers-families.html)
[81] Maria Abi-Habib, "Jihadists Extend Control Into Lebanese City," *The Wall Street Journal.* August 3, 2014. (http://online.wsj.com/articles/jihadists-extend-control-into-lebanese-city-1407109896?mod=wsj_india_main http://www.assafir.com/Article/365429/RelatedArticle)
[82] "بيروت: تدابير لمنع تهريب «السجناء الإسلاميين»," *Asharq Al-Awsat* (Saudi Arabia), July 4, 2014. (http://www.aawsat.com/home/article/130836)
[83] "اللبنانيين العسكريين إطلاق مقابل نساء 5و دولار مليون 30 .<النصرة> مع تبادل صفقة" *Asharq al-Awsat (UK),* June 24, 2015. (http://goo.gl/hpg79j); "Lebanon and Nusra 'hostage exchange' reaches final steps," *al-Araby al-Jadeed (UK),* August 5, 2015. (http://www.alaraby.co.uk/english/news/2015/8/5/lebanese-army-general-announces-end-of-negotiations-with-nusra)
[84] U.S. Treasury Department, "Treasury Designates Twelve Foreign Terrorist Fighter Facilitators," September 24, 2014. (http://www.treasury.gov/press-center/press-releases/Pages/jl2651.aspx); Andrew Gilligan, "Minister's Family Ties to Terror," *The Telegraph (UK).* November 1, 2014. (http://www.telegraph.co.uk/news/worldnews/middleeast/qatar/11203140/Ministers-family-ties-to-terror.html)
[85] Ellen Knickmeyer, "Al Qaeda-Linked Groups Increasingly Funded by Ransom," *Wall Street Journal,* July 29, 2014. (http://www.wsj.com/articles/ransom-fills-terrorist-coffers-1406637010)

David Andrew Weinberg   November 17, 2015

gesture to families in need. However, it is difficult to explain why Qatar has been freelancing in so many of these crises without also recognizing how this fits into Doha's broader efforts to turn money and extremist connections into political power, even if doing so inevitably results in the strengthening of violent extremists who act in the service of al-Qaeda.

Qatar craves the international spotlight, has petrodollars to spare, and maintains a panoply of unsavory contacts in the world of Islamist extremists. The Persian Gulf states pay for public relations in the West all the time – Qatar just seems to be cutting to the chase through buying headlines and the gratitude of countries whose citizens have been kidnapped via negotiating and allegedly paying ransoms to terrorist groups. Doha has long sought political influence by brokering accords between Western nations, regional powers, and terrorist groups, and we know that it has often greased the wheels, at least for that kind of accord, with a healthy infusion of Qatari cash.

It becomes far more difficult to trust Qatar's motives for mediating hostage releases once one understands how negligent the Qataris have been with regard to some of these same terrorist groups. Qatar was originally announced as a nominal member of the anti-IS airpower coalition but apparently has yet to launch a single strike against the group.[86] It also has yet to even press charges against individuals living in or visiting its territory who are under U.N. sanctions for allegedly funding IS's forerunner, al-Qaeda in Iraq.[87]

Doha has similarly yet to press charges against individuals under U.S. or U.N. sanctions on charges of funding the Nusra Front or other branches of al-Qaeda.[88] According to American and Arab officials who were cited by the *Wall Street Journal*, Qatar even let commanders of the Nusra Front into its territory to facilitate such fundraising and for meetings with Qatari military officials.[89] American officials up to the level of President Obama himself have reportedly chided the Qataris

---

[86] Helene Cooper and Eric Schmitt, "Airstrikes by U.S. and Allies Hit ISIS Targets in Syria," *New York Times*, September 22, 2014. (http://www.nytimes.com/2014/09/23/world/middleeast/us-and-allies-hit-isis-targets-in-syria.html); Peter Kovessy, "Qatar Supports Syria Aerial Bombing, but Urges Non-Military Solution," *Doha News (Qatar)*, September 25, 2014. (http://dohanews.co/qatar-flies-alongside-gcc-states-syria-bombing-urges-world-go-beyond-military-action/); U.S. Defense Department, "Operation Inherent Resolve: Targeted Operations against ISIL Terrorists," *Defense Department website*, accessed November 12, 2015. (http://www.defense.gov/News/Special-Reports/0814_Inherent-Resolve)

[87] David Andrew Weinberg, *Qatar and Terror Finance – Part I: Negligence*, FDD Press. December 2014. (http://www.defenddemocracy.org/content/uploads/publications/Qatar_Part_I.pdf); Jamie Dettmer, "An American Ally's Grand Mosque of Hate," *Daily Beast*, February 19, 2015.
(http://www.thedailybeast.com/articles/2015/02/19/qatar-s-a-us-ally-against-isis-so-why-s-it-cheerleading-the-bad-guys.html); David Andrew Weinberg, "UN Official Reportedly Meets with Iraqi on al Qaeda Sanctions List," *Long War Journal*, October 30, 2015. (http://www.longwarjournal.org/archives/2015/10/un-official-reportedly-meets-with-iraqi-on-al-qaeda-sanctions-list.php)

[88] David Andrew Weinberg, "Qatar and Terror Finance – Part I: Negligence," *Foundation for Defense of Democracies Press*, December 2014.
(http://www.defenddemocracy.org/content/uploads/publications/Qatar_Part_I.pdf); David Andrew Weinberg, "Analysis: Qatar Still Negligent on Terror Finance," *Long War Journal*, August 19, 2015.
(http://www.longwarjournal.org/archives/2015/08/analysis-qatar-still-negligent-on-terror-finance.php)

[89] Jay Solomon and Nour Malas, "Qatar's Ties to Militants Strain Alliance: The Persian Gulf State's Relationships in the Region are Both Useful and a Worry to the U.S.," *Wall Street Journal*, February 23, 2015.
(http://www.wsj.com/articles/qatars-ties-to-militants-strain-alliance-1424748601?alg=y)

David Andrew Weinberg   November 17, 2015

for letting weapons fall into the hands of the Nusra Front, so it seems consistent that Doha might also be inclined to let ransoms flow to the group.[90]

Qatar's reckless enthusiasm for mediating hostage deals with terrorists seems to be supercharging the profits that these groups receive as a result of KFR. Rather than shifting the blame back and forth, it is clear that both Europe and Qatar must do better. Yet there is no reason to believe that anything will improve until Washington exerts new pressure on our irresponsible allies to sufficiently motivate better behavior.

U.S. Policy:

Although the U.S. and British governments do not pay ransoms, the exchange of Bowe Bergdahl for five Taliban commanders last year strained the administration's insistence that America's policy is "to refuse the payment of ransoms or make other concessions to hostage-takers."[91] Like the arms-for-hostages trade included as part of the Reagan team's Iran-Contra debacle, the Bergdahl trade has created confusion about America's no concessions policy and likely whet the appetite of the terror masters. Indeed, anecdotal evidence suggests that government concessions to terrorists ultimately beget more kidnappings and inflated demands.

The brother of executed U.S. hostage Kayla Mueller believes the Bergdahl swap persuaded IS to increase what it demanded in exchange for Kayla's release.[92] According to the _Daily Beast_, Qatar's proposed exchange of the Huang couple for admitted al-Qaeda sleeper agent Ali Saleh al-Marri was floated in July 2014, two months after Bergdahl's release, "rais[ing] troubling questions about whether the Bergdahl trade opened a kind of Pandora's box, signaling to foreign governments that they can pressure the United States to make concessions on terrorism by trading American prisoners abroad for dangerous extremists held in the United States."[93] According to _Reuters_, the Taliban's chief negotiator in the Bergdahl swap "noted at one point during the talks that Israel had traded more than 1,000 prisoners for a single Israeli soldier" in order to justify his insistence on all five high-value Taliban detainees being part of the eventual prisoner release.[94] According to a former hostage of IS in Syria, "the kidnappers knew which countries would be the most amenable

[90] Mark Mazzetti, C. J. Chivers, and Eric Schmitt. "Taking Outsize Role in Syria, Qatar Funnels Arms to Rebels." _New York Times_, June 29, 2013. (http://www.nytimes.com/2013/06/30/world/middleeast/sending-missiles-to-syrian-rebels-qatar-muscles-in.html)

[91] U.S. Treasury Department, "Remarks of Under Secretary for Terrorism and Financial Intelligence David S. Cohen at The Carnegie Endowment For International Peace, "Attacking ISIL's Financial Foundation," October 23, 2014. (http://www.treasury.gov/press-center/press-releases/Pages/jl2672.aspx)

[92] "Jesuit Priest Prem Kumar Contradicts Govt Story: Did India Pay Taliban for his Release?" _First Post_, March 5, 2015. (http://www.firstpost.com/politics/jesuit-priest-prem-kumar-contradicts-govt-story-did-india-pay-taliban-for-his-release-2137115.html)

[93] Shane Harris and James Kirchick, "Exclusive: Freed Al Qaeda Agent Was Part of Proposed Swap for Jailed Americans," _Daily Beast_, January 25, 2015. (http://www.thedailybeast.com/articles/2015/01/25/exclusive-freed-al-qaeda-agent-was-part-of-proposed-swap-for-jailed-americans.html)

[94] Steve Holland and Warren Strobel, "Inside the White House's Decision to Free Bergdahl," _Reuters_, June 4, 2014. (http://www.reuters.com/article/2014/06/05/us-usa-bergdahl-obama-insight-idUSKBN0EG04720140605#1D2gSdLwmSo0515y.97)

David Andrew Weinberg   November 17, 2015

to their demands" and "started with the Spanish" because they said Madrid paid €6 million to al-Qaeda for hostages seized in Mauritania.[95]

The administration wishfully claims that by not paying ransoms, we deter the kidnapping of Americans abroad.[96] Yet observers have also raised serious questions about the accuracy of this admittedly appealing wish. David Rohde, a Pulitzer Prize-winning reporter who was kidnapped by the Taliban and later escaped, concludes: "I've seen no clear evidence that groups are grabbing more Europeans and fewer Americans... they take any foreigners they can get and use the Europeans for ransom and the Americans for publicity."[97] Rather, there are other, more persuasive reasons the U.S. government should not pay these ransoms, most notably the benefit that disbursements of such a scale would likely confer to violent jihadists.

Overall, it also is worth recognizing that the Obama administration adopted many sensible new measures this June as a result of its presidentially-mandated review of U.S. hostage policy.

Those measures include: (1) reaffirming America's "longstanding commitment to make no concessions to individuals or groups holding U.S. Nationals hostage," most notably by reiterating that the U.S. government will not itself pay ransoms; (2) committing to work closely with hostages' families and to "proactively share as much information as possible" with them; (3) making clear that the U.S. "does not intend to add to families' pain... by suggesting that they could face criminal prosecution;" and (4) authorizing government officials to assist families if they choose to communicate with hostage-takers so as to provide assistance with safety and reducing the risk of being defrauded.[98]

In addition, President Obama approved a new executive order to streamline the executive branch's responsiveness to kidnapping threats, creating: (1) a Hostage Recovery Fusion Cell based at the FBI in order to serve as American's full-time, operational eyes and ears on this issue; (2) a senior-level interagency Hostage Response Group chaired by NSC staff to provide policy guidance to the President on KFR cases and U.S. strategy; (3) an Intelligence Community Issue Manager for Hostage affairs in the office of the DNI to prioritize intelligence collection and dissemination in cases of Americans being held overseas; and (4) a Special Presidential Envoy for Hostage Affairs based at the State Department to handle diplomatic outreach with regard to ongoing hostage crises.[99]

---

[95] Rukmini Callimachi, "The Horror before the Beheadings: ISIS Hostages Endured Torture and Dashed Hopes, Freed Cellmates Say," *New York Times*, October 25, 2014.
(http://www.nytimes.com/2014/10/26/world/middleeast/horror-before-the-beheadings-what-isis-hostages-endured-in-syria.html?_r=0)
[96] U.S. Treasury Department, "Remarks of Under Secretary for Terrorism and Financial Intelligence David S. Cohen at The Carnegie Endowment For International Peace, 'Attacking ISIL's Financial Foundation,'" October 23, 2014.
(http://www.treasury.gov/press-center/press-releases/Pages/jl2672.aspx)
[97] Quoted in Margaret Sullivan, "Covering Hostages, without Becoming Pawns," *New York Times*, April 4, 2015.
(http://www.nytimes.com/2015/04/05/public-editor/covering-hostages-without-becoming-pawns.html)
[98] White House, *Report on U.S. Hostage Policy*, June 2015, pp. 6-7.
(https://www.whitehouse.gov/sites/default/files/docs/report_on_us_hostage_policy_final.pdf)
[99] President Barack Obama, "Executive Order 13698 – Hostage Recovery Activities," *White House website*, June 24, 2015. (https://www.whitehouse.gov/the-press-office/2015/06/24/executive-order-and-presidential-policy-directive-hostage-recovery)

David Andrew Weinberg   November 17, 2015

~~Now that these new contours of U.S. policy have been set, the most important thing Congress can do would be to focus on reducing the volume of ransom payments that reach terrorist organizations, primarily by discouraging the governments of U.S. allies that seem to be the biggest source of such skyrocketing payments.~~ Indeed, while the Hostage Review Team's 24 "Major Findings and Recommendations" included numerous recommendations on how to improve U.S. government coordination, engage with families and external stakeholders, and boost intelligence sharing and collection, this list does not seem to have included a single new recommendation for how to stop other governments from continuing to pay large ransoms to terrorist groups.[100]

Policy Recommendations on Combating Kidnapping for Ransom:

There are smart steps that Congress can take to help decrease terrorists' ill-gotten profits from kidnapping and to mitigate the harm that this practice causes the American people:

1. Penalize Governments that Pay. The U.S. has worked hard in concert with Britain to pass measures that condemn the payment of ransom to terrorists at a variety of fora, including the U.N. Security Council, the G8, the OSCE, and the Global Counterterrorism Forum, in which most our European and Gulf allies are members. Yet that apparently has not been enough to deter the payment of state ransoms, since many of the alleged episodes described in my testimony today have occurred after the passage of these resolutions. Thus, the U.S. needs to take new measures to penalize foreign governments that pay ransoms, even if it is only through reputational damage by publicly identifying and condemning such irresponsible conduct. This could include mandating an annual standalone report or a new section in an existing report to publicly shame those governments that the executive branch believes paid direct or indirect ransoms to terrorists. It could also include the imposition of banking sanctions or statutory penalties such as being designated a "jurisdiction of primary money laundering concern," facing tougher criteria or licensing rules for military sales or bilateral investments, ineligibility for bilateral free trade agreements and U.S. backing at the U.N., or even sanctions on foreign governmental institutions or officials who authorized such payments to terrorists.

2. Instruct U.S. Diplomats to Prioritize Stopping State Ransoms. On behalf of the President, Secretary of State Kerry should be encouraged to instruct our pertinent diplomats to make a priority of persuading U.S. allies to stop the direct or indirect payment of ransoms by governments to terrorists. Relevant diplomats who should be tasked with this instruction should include not just the new Special Presidential Envoy for Hostage Affairs but also our ambassadors in several key Gulf and European capitals. Members of Congress could also be raising this issue with State Department officials who cover the regions of Europe and the Near East who testify on the Hill and pressing administration officials to articulate a viable new strategy that goes beyond mere cheap talk and norm-articulation for convincing our allies to stop this destructive behavior.

3. Directly Engage with Legislators and Other Officials Abroad. Congress could call on legislators and other policy-makers in foreign countries, especially those countries that are believed to have repeatedly paid ransoms to terrorists, and encourage them to pass legislation and

---

[100] White House, "Annex A: Major Findings and Recommendations of the Hostage Review Team," *Report on U.S. Hostage Policy*, June 2015, pp. 12-19.
(https://www.whitehouse.gov/sites/default/files/docs/report_on_us_hostage_policy_final.pdf)

David Andrew Weinberg   November 17, 2015

other policy directives condemning or outlawing the payment of direct or indirect ransoms to terrorist groups. Such regulations could also legally adopt new measures for addressing KFR, such as the best practices for combating KFR listed in the Global Counterterrorism Forum's 2012 Algiers Memorandum.[101]

4. Go After the Middlemen. Particularly after a ransom has been paid, U.S. officials should, when possible, target the facilitators that profited off of the ransom or enabled the kidnapping to occur. For example, terrorists frequently outsource the actual act of kidnapping Westerners to other armed groups, tribes, or criminal networks in order to reduce the risk to their own operatives.[102] These accomplices should be held accountable for the deadly consequences of their actions through legal or even military means.

5. Ensure Justice is Served. While it should not be allowed to take priority over seeking the safe return of Americans held hostage overseas, our government should also ensure that all worthwhile efforts are being exerted to bring those terrorists who use KFR to justice. Simply adding the kidnappers onto a sanctions list is not enough. While pursuing judgments against kidnappers in U.S. courts, Washington should also work with – and when necessary, pressure – allied governments to help enact justice on the ground. This should also be a key goal of American military or intelligence activities in various conflict zones such as Iraq, Syria, or Yemen. Achieving this objective may require additional bureaucratic reorganization or new dedicated staff positions to focus on the day after and keeping onetime kidnappers from becoming repeat offenders.

6. Stop Hostage-Takers from Enjoying the Benefits of Completed Ransoms. The U.S. government should have dedicated staff whose job is to keep terrorists from enjoying the benefits of ransoms that have already been paid. Just because a terrorist group like IS or al-Qaeda may have cash in hand does not necessarily mean that it must be permitted to spend it freely, and treating this objective as a constant and well-funded priority would help reduce the benefits that terrorist groups are able to reap from KFR. U.S. officials should continue to focus on making it harder to smuggle sensitive goods such as powerful vehicles and weaponry into territory held by terrorists and work to block their use of financial institutions for moving received ransoms in order to force terrorists to engage in vulnerable courier missions instead. The U.S. should also hold foreign governments that pay ransoms accountable for helping seize back those funds and track down kidnappers in order to reduce the harm that those states' actions have caused.

7. Consider Limiting Reimbursements of Terrorist Ransoms by Insurance Firms. While governments seem to be fueling the recent increase in ransoms paid to terrorist groups, insurance companies also represent a concentrated group of actors with the capability to unintentionally fuel such terrorist activities through multimillion dollar payouts. Lawrence Wright of the *New Yorker* noted in his thoughtful analysis of the human toll of KFR by terrorists that "corporations routinely

---

[101] Global Counterterrorism Forum, "Algiers Memorandum on Good Practices on Preventing and Denying the Benefits of Kidnapping for Ransom by Terrorists," April 2012.
(https://www.thegctf.org/documents/10162/159874/Algiers+Memorandum-English.pdf)
[102] United Nations, "Sixteenth Report of the Analytical Support and Sanctions Monitoring Team submitted pursuant to resolution 2161 (2014) concerning Al-Qaida and associated individuals and entities," September 29, 2014.
(http://www.un.org/ga/search/view_doc.asp?symbol=S/2014/770)

David Andrew Weinberg   November 17, 2015

take out ransom insurance for employees stationed abroad."[103] Our British allies recently passed a law that criminalizes payments from insurance companies to reimburse ransom payments to terrorists.[104] Congress and the executive branch could explore whether phasing in a similar ban or certain limits on insurance payouts could reduce the size of ransoms that flow to terrorist groups if it can be done in a manner that avoids imposing an undue additional burden on the employers or families of kidnapping victims who simply want to bring American citizens home.

8. Mitigate the Harm Caused to U.S. Citizens. Even when U.S. hostages are able to make it home, the harm caused to them and their families is immense. Journalist Matt Schrier escaped from a Nusra Front prison in 2013 where he had been repeatedly tortured, and he expressed deep disappointment with the level of support he received from the U.S. government.[105] For instance, he reportedly told *McClatchy* that "the FBI has made it impossible for me to recover," providing inconsistent mental health care, forcing Schrier to pay for his flight home even though his captors had cleaned out his bank account, and suggesting he stay in a homeless shelter when he had trouble getting a new ID and Social Security number because al-Qaeda stole his identity.[106] Some of the problems Schrier encountered after coming home could be addressed by the administration's new policies, if properly implemented. But given that these policies clearly leave open a door for victims' families to pay multi-million dollar ransoms, we should recognize that new American policies could unintentionally force victims of terrorism and their families into destitution. Legislative and executive branch officials may therefore wish explore whether to set up a dedicated fund with seized terrorist assets to compensate the victims of kidnappings and similar violent acts by terror groups for the damages and suffering imposed. However, such a fund would likely have to be disbursed without consideration of whether a ransom was paid in order to avoid creating a moral hazard problem that would incentivize larger payouts.

Part II. Negligence by U.S. Allies against Private Terror Finance

On last year's anniversary of 9/11, Secretary of State John Kerry gathered in Jeddah to meet with his counterparts from Turkey and ten Arab countries. With some considerable effort, he elicited from all but one of his counterparts a pledge to take new steps against terrorism and terror finance as a key part of their contribution to the multilateral coalition against IS. Turkey was the only participant not mentioned in the declaration, known as the Jeddah Communiqué, although a senior Turkish official told *Reuters* this was because Ankara was engaged at the time in sensitive

---

[103] Lawrence Wright, "Five Hostages," *The New Yorker*, July 6, 2015.
(http://www.newyorker.com/magazine/2015/07/06/five-hostages)
[104] U.K. Government, "Counter-Terrorism and Security Act 2015," chap. 6, pt. 6, sec. 42: "Insurance against Payments Made in Response to Terrorist Demands," *Legislation.Gov.UK*. as enacted February 12, 2015.
(http://www.legislation.gov.uk/ukpga/2015/6/section/42/enacted)
[105] C. J. Chivers, "American Tells of Odyssey as Prisoner of Syrian Rebels," *New York Times*, August 22, 2013.
(http://www.nytimes.com/2013/08/23/world/middleeast/american-tells-of-odyssey-as-prisoner-of-syrian-rebels.html)
[106] Nancy A. Youssef, "Former al Qaida Hostage Recounts Nightmare of Dealing with FBI," *McClatchy*, November 28, 2014. (http://www.mcclatchydc.com/news/nation-world/national/national-security/article24776860.html)

David Andrew Weinberg   November 17, 2015

negotiations with IS over the release of forty-six Turkish hostages being held in Mosul.[107] Since then, all of those hostages were released in a trade that reportedly saw Turkey release 180 individuals linked to IS from Turkish jails and hospitals against U.S. wishes.[108] However, Turkey has pledged to combat terrorist finance in a variety of other multilateral settings as well.[109]

The Jeddah Communiqué committed many of America's most important Middle Eastern allies to "stopping the flow of foreign fighters through neighboring countries, countering financing of ISIL and other violent extremists, repudiating their hateful ideology, ending impunity and bringing perpetrators to justice."[110] Yet as I testified before Congress in July, many of these states failed to follow through on their commitments to combat hate speech, tackle terror finance, and end the impunity of its practitioners. Sadly, Qatar, Kuwait, Saudi Arabia, and Turkey have all failed in some of these important regards.[111]

Qatar:

Last year U.S. officials identified Qatar along with Kuwait as one of two "permissive jurisdictions" for terror finance in the Gulf Cooperation Council (GCC), a region that has been the largest source of private donations to al-Qaeda's senior leadership in Pakistan.[112] Since then, Kuwait has at least pursued some terror finance court cases, something Qatar still has yet to do. Doha seems to be a place where financiers of al-Qaeda, IS, and Hamas enjoy legal impunity.

Treasury also revealed last year that IS's "Amir of suicide bombers... arranged to receive approximately $2 million from a Qatar-based ISIL financial facilitator" for military operations in 2013.[113] There is no indication that Qatar punished the individual in question, who the U.S. claims "also enlisted [the ISIL official's] assistance with fundraising efforts in Qatar."[114]

The U.S. government's top official for combating terrorist finance revealed in October 2014 that Khalifa al-Subaiy and Abdulrahman al-Nu'aymi, individuals under U.S. and U.N. terror finance

---

[107] Jason Szep, "U.S. Wins Arab Support for Syria/Iraq Military Campaign," *Reuters*, September 12, 2014. (http://www.reuters.com/article/2014/09/12/us-iraq-crisis-kerry-idUSKBN0H50MA20140912#Y0tOfEC8IHo1iLg8.97)

[108] Costanze Letsch and Ewen MacAskill, "Turkey Freed British Jihadis in Swap Deal for ISIS Hostages – Reports," *The Guardian (UK)*, October 6, 2014. (http://www.theguardian.com/world/2014/oct/06/turkey-britons-swap-deal-isis-hostages-reports)

[109] G20, "Communiqué: G20 Finance Ministers and Central Bank Governors Meeting," September 4 & 5, 2015. (https://g20.org/wp-content/uploads/2015/09/September-FMCBG-Communique.pdf)

[110] U.S. State Department, "Jeddah Communiqué," September 11, 2014. (http://www.state.gov/r/pa/prs/ps/2014/09/231496.htm)

[111] David Andrew Weinberg. "The Gulf Cooperation Council Camp David Summit: Any Results?" *Testimony before the House Committee on Foreign Affairs Subcommittee on the Middle East and North Africa*, July 9, 2015. (http://docs.house.gov/meetings/FA/FA13/20150709/103726/HHRG-114-FA13-Wstate-WeinbergD-20150709.pdf)

[112] U.S. Treasury Department, "Remarks of Under Secretary for Terrorism and Financial Intelligence David Cohen before the Center for a New American Security on 'Confronting New Threats in Terrorist Financing,'" March 4, 2014. (http://www.treasury.gov/press-center/press-releases/Pages/jl2308.aspx)

[113] U.S. Treasury Department, "Treasury Designates Twelve Foreign Terrorist Fighter Facilitators," September 24, 2014. (http://www.treasury.gov/press-center/press-releases/Pages/jl2651.aspx)

[114] U.S. Treasury Department, "Treasury Designates Twelve Foreign Terrorist Fighter Facilitators," September 24, 2014. (http://www.treasury.gov/press-center/press-releases/Pages/jl2651.aspx)

David Andrew Weinberg   November 17, 2015

sanctions, were living in Qatar but "have not been acted against under Qatari law."[115] Given that Nu'aymi is accused by Treasury of having funded the organization we now know as IS back when it was al-Qaeda in Iraq at a rate of over $2 million a month,[116] one would think that punishing him would top Doha's list of priorities as part of the anti-IS coalition to deter future acts of terror finance. Treasury alleges that Subaiy was a financier of Khalid Sheikh Muhammad, al-Qaeda's mastermind of the 9/11 attacks.[117] Despite Qatari claims that Subaiy would be "under control" and his finances controlled or supervised,[118] he later resumed sending hundreds of thousands of dollars intended for al-Qaeda in Pakistan, according to the U.S. government.[119]

Qatar has also hosted on its territory and declined to take legal action against two other individuals whom the U.N. sanctioned on charges of funding al-Qaeda's Iraqi offshoot: Hamid Abdullah al-Ali and Muthanna Harith al-Dhari.[120] Both cases would seem to represent violations of a U.N. travel ban. Qatar's Father Emir was even caught on videotape hugging and kissing the latter individual while visiting him this year in Jordan.[121]

Many of these cases of terror financiers enjoying impunity in Qatar have a KFR tie-in as well.

First, the Taliban asserted two of its officials were able to visit Qatar for a week to meet members of the Taliban five swapped for Sgt. Bergdahl; the group also claimed that the two men were then allowed to depart Qatar before they were detained in Bahrain and extradited into Kabul's custody.[122] Afghan officials told the *Wall Street Journal* that one of the two captured men was "in charge of fundraising for the network," and the *New York Times* reported that his prominence had grown "through his fund-raising work in gulf countries" according to U.S. and Afghan officials.[123]

---

[115] Robert Mendick, "Terror Financiers are Living Freely in Qatar, US Discloses," *The Telegraph (UK)*, November 16, 2014. (http://www.telegraph.co.uk/news/worldnews/islamic-state/11233407/Terror-financiers-are-living-freely-in-Qatar-US-discloses.html)
[116] U.S. Treasury Department, "Treasury Designates Al-Qa'ida Supporters in Qatar and Yemen," December 18, 2013. (http://www.treasury.gov/press-center/press-releases/Pages/jl2249.aspx)
[117] U.S. Treasury Department, "Treasury Designates Gulf-Based al Qaida Financiers," June 5, 2008. (http://www.treasury.gov/press-center/press-releases/Pages/hp1011.aspx)
[118] David Andrew Weinberg, *Qatar and Terror Finance Part I: Negligence*, FDD Press, December 2014. (http://www.defenddemocracy.org/content/uploads/publications/Qatar_Part_I.pdf)
[119] U.S. Treasury Department, "Treasury Designates Twelve Foreign Terrorist Fighter Facilitators," September 24, 2014. (http://www.treasury.gov/press-center/press-releases/Pages/jl2651.aspx)
[120] Andrew Gilligan, "The 'Club Med for Terrorists'," *The Telegraph (UK)*, September 27, 2014. (http://www.telegraph.co.uk/news/worldnews/middleeast/qatar/11125897/The-Club-Med-for-terrorists.html); David Andrew Weinberg, "UN Official Reportedly Meets with Iraqi on al Qaeda Sanctions List," *Long War Journal*, October 30, 2015. (http://www.longwarjournal.org/archives/2015/10/un-official-reportedly-meets-with-iraqi-on-al-qaeda-sanctions-list.php)
[121] David Andrew Weinberg, "UN Official Reportedly Meets with Iraqi on al Qaeda Sanctions List," *Long War Journal*, October 30, 2015. (http://www.longwarjournal.org/archives/2015/10/un-official-reportedly-meets-with-iraqi-on-al-qaeda-sanctions-list.php)
[122] Thomas Joscelyn, "Taliban Claims Captured Haqqani Leaders Visited ex-Gitmo Detainees in Qatar," *Long War Journal*, October 19, 2014. (http://www.longwarjournal.org/archives/2014/10/taliban_claims_captu.php); "Statement of Islamic Emirate regarding the Arrest of Anas Haqqani and Hafiz Abdul Rasheed," *Islamic Emirate of Afghanistan website*, October 18, 2014, archived October 20, 2014. (https://web.archive.org/web/20141020045321/http://shahamat-english.com/index.php/paighamoona/50407-statement-of-islamic-emirate-regarding-the-arrest-of-anas-haqqani-and-hafiz-abdul-rasheed)
[123] Magherita Stancati and Eshanullah Amiri, "Haqqani Leaders Detained in Persian Gulf, not inside Afghanistan," *Wall Street Journal*, October 19, 2014. (http://online.wsj.com/articles/haqqani-leaders-detained-in-persian-gulf-not-

David Andrew Weinberg   November 17, 2015

Qatar has long been described as a source of concern over private finance reaching terror groups in Afghanistan such as al-Qaeda, the Taliban, and the Haqqani network.[124]

Second, this August the U.S. imposed sanctions on charges of funding al-Qaeda against two Qatari nationals who ran what was arguably the country's largest fundraising campaign for Syria. Treasury indicated that one of the men, Sa'd bin Sa'd al-Ka'bi, had been requested by the Nusra Front to "act as an intermediary for collecting a ransom for a hostage being held by ANF [i.e. Nusra], and al-Ka'bi worked to facilitate a ransom payment in exchange for the release of a hostage held by ANF."[125] According to al-Arabiya, U.S. officials who briefed reporters on Ka'bi's role in al-Qaeda ransoms "refused to answer a question on whether the Qatari government itself may have contributed to the financing of ransoms for any kidnapped persons."[126] His campaign continued to operate in Qatar for nearly a year after it was reportedly endorsed on social media by the Nusra Front in August 2013,[127] and in August 2015 a senior Obama administration official indicated that Qatar still "has not arrested the two men."[128]

Third, among the al-Qaeda operatives that Nusra has tried to get released from Lebanon's Roumieh Prison in deals that had Qatari mediation is 'Abd al-Malik 'Abd al-Salam, also known as the Wolf of al-Qaeda or Umar al-Qatari.[129] According to the U.S. government, 'Abd al-Salam is a Jordanian national with a Qatari ID card and a long history of funding al-Qaeda, including in collaboration with Qatari nationals also under U.S. and U.N. sanctions.[130]

Treasury noted that "in May 2012, Umar al-Qatari was apprehended by Lebanese authorities in Beirut as he attempted to depart for Qatar. At the time of his arrest he was carrying thousands of

inside-afghanistan-1413733878); Declan Walsh, "2 Haqqani Militant Leaders are Captured, Afghan Officials Say," *New York Times*, October 16, 2014. (http://www.nytimes.com/2014/10/17/world/asia/haqqani-leaders-arrested-afghanistan-khost.html?_r=0)

[124] "Terrorist Finance: Action Request for Senior Level Engagement on Terrorism Finance," *Wikileaks*, December 30, 2009. (https://wikileaks.org/plusd/cables/09STATE131801_a.html); U.S. Treasury Department, "Under Secretary Cohen to Visit Qatar, United Arab Emirates, and Saudi Arabia on May 20-26, 2013," May 20, 2013. (http://www.treasury.gov/press-center/media-advisories/Pages/05202013b.aspx); David Andrew Weinberg, *Qatar and Terror Finance – Part I: Negligence*, FDD Press, December 2014. (http://www.defenddemocracy.org/content/uploads/publications/Qatar_Part_I.pdf)

[125] U.S. Treasury Department, "U.S. Designates Financial Supporters of Al-Qaida and Al-Nusrah Front," August 5, 2014. (http://www.treasury.gov/press-center/press-releases/Pages/jl0143.aspx)

[126] Muna Shikaki, "U.S. Targets Alleged Qatari Militant Backers," *Al Arabiya (UAE)*, August 5, 2015. (http://english.alarabiya.net/en/News/middle-east/2015/08/05/U-S-targets-alleged-Qatari-financiers-of-Al-Nusra-and-Al-Qaeda.html)

[127] David Andrew Weinberg, "Analysis: Qatar Still Negligent on Terror Finance," *Long War Journal*, August 19, 2015. (http://www.longwarjournal.org/archives/2015/08/analysis-qatar-still-negligent-on-terror-finance.php); Joby Warrick, "Syrian Conflict said to Fuel Sectarian Tensions in Persian Gulf," *Washington Post*, December 18, 2013. (https://www.washingtonpost.com/world/national-security/syrian-conflict-said-to-fuel-sectarian-tensions-in-persian-gulf/2013/12/18/c160ad82-6831-11e3-8b5b-a77187b716a3_story.html)

[128] Taimur Khan, "US Names Two Qatari Nationals as Financiers of Terrorism," *The National (UAE)*, August 6, 2015. (http://www.thenational.ae/world/americas/us-names-two-qatari-nationals-as-financiers-of-terrorism)

[129] U.S. Treasury Department, "Treasury Designates Twelve Foreign Terrorist Fighter Facilitators," September 24, 2014. (http://www.treasury.gov/press-center/press-releases/Pages/jl2651.aspx); "صقر يتوسط لإطلاق «الذئب»," *Al-Akhbar (Lebanon)*, January 17, 2014. (http://www.al-akhbar.com/node/175702)

[130] U.S. Treasury Department, "Treasury Designates Twelve Foreign Terrorist Fighter Facilitators," September 24, 2014. (http://www.treasury.gov/press-center/press-releases/Pages/jl2651.aspx)

David Andrew Weinberg   November 17, 2015

dollars intended for al-Qaida."[131] Press reports claim that the person who gave him the funds was Abdulaziz al-Attiyah, a Qatari arrested in Lebanon in 2012 on terror-related charges after a tip from Washington, according to U.S. and Lebanese officials.[132] He was reportedly convicted of terror finance in Lebanon in 2014, but it was in absentia because he had been freed from detention and his travel ban lifted, allegedly due to intense Qatari diplomatic pressure.[133]

Meanwhile, the Nusra Front's 'Abd al-Salam appears to be the son of a recently killed jihadist leader[134] who allegedly was supported by Qatari intelligence,[135] fought for al-Qaeda in Iraq, and purportedly gave material support to Iraqi *mujahideen* from Qatar[136] before founding Jund al-Aqsa. The Jund is a Syrian jihadist force that received considerable funding from private Gulf donors[137] but is banned as a terrorist group by Britain and splintered off from Nusra for refusing to fight IS.[138] It openly voices backing for Ayman al-Zawahiri[139] and has been called an al-Qaeda front[140] whose battlefield activities were directed by an official of al-Qaeda's Khorasan cell.[141]

Kuwait:

Last year, the Treasury Department described Kuwait along with Qatar as one of the Gulf's "permissive jurisdictions" for terrorist finance and revealed that Kuwait had become the top source

---

[131] U.S. Treasury Department. "Treasury Designates Twelve Foreign Terrorist Fighter Facilitators," September 24, 2014. (http://www.treasury.gov/press-center/press-releases/Pages/jl2651.aspx)

[132] Andrew Gilligan, "Minister's Family Ties to Terror," *The Telegraph (UK)*, November 1, 2014. (http://www.telegraph.co.uk/news/worldnews/middleeast/qatar/11203140/Ministers-family-ties-to-terror.html); Jay Solomon and Nour Malas. "Qatar's Ties to Militants Strain Alliance: The Persian Gulf State's Relationships in the Region are Both Useful and a Worry to the U.S.," *Wall Street Journal*, February 23, 2015. (http://www.wsj.com/articles/qatars-ties-to-militants-strain-alliance-1424748601?alg=y);

[133] Andrew Gilligan, "Minister's Family Ties to Terror," *The Telegraph (UK)*, November 1, 2014. (http://www.telegraph.co.uk/news/worldnews/middleeast/qatar/11203140/Ministers-family-ties-to-terror.html); Jay Solomon and Nour Malas. "Qatar's Ties to Militants Strain Alliance: The Persian Gulf State's Relationships in the Region are Both Useful and a Worry to the U.S.," *Wall Street Journal*, February 23, 2015. (http://www.wsj.com/articles/qatars-ties-to-militants-strain-alliance-1424748601?alg=y);

[134] David Andrew Weinberg. "The Gulf Cooperation Council Camp David Summit: Any Results?" *Testimony before the House Committee on Foreign Affairs Subcommittee on the Middle East and North Africa*, July 9, 2015. (http://docs.house.gov/meetings/FA/FA13/20150709/103726/HHRG-114-FA13-Wstate-WeinbergD-20150709.pdf)

[135] "الجيش الحر يبدأ الإستلاء على تنظيم مسلح تابع لقطر," *Al Hadath News* (Lebanon), May 4, 2014. (http://www.alhadathnews.net/archives/120979)

[136] David Andrew Weinberg. "The Gulf Cooperation Council Camp David Summit: Any Results?" *Testimony before the House Committee on Foreign Affairs Subcommittee on the Middle East and North Africa*, July 9, 2015. (http://docs.house.gov/meetings/FA/FA13/20150709/103726/HHRG-114-FA13-Wstate-WeinbergD-20150709.pdf)

[137] Tam Hussein, "Why did Jund al-Aqsa Join Nusra Front in Taking Out 'Moderate' Rebels in Idlib," *Huffington Post*, June 11, 2014, updated June 1, 2015. (http://www.huffingtonpost.co.uk/tam-hussein/nusra-front_b_6112790.html?utm_hp_ref=uk-news)

[138] U.K. Government, "The Terrorism Act 2000 (Proscribed Organisations) (Amendment) Order 2015," *Legislation.Gov.UK*, coming into force January 23, 2015. (http://www.legislation.gov.uk/uksi/2015/55/pdfs/uksi_20150055_en.pdf)

[139] Aymenn Jawad al-Tamimi, "Jund al-Aqsa Withdraws from Jaish al-Fatah," *Jihad Intel*, Middle East Forum, October 24, 2015. (http://jihadintel.meforum.org/189/jund-al-aqsa-withdraws-from-jaysh-al-fatah)

[140] Thomas Joscelyn. "An al Qaeda Front Group in Syria," *Long War Journal*, May 2, 2015. (http://www.longwarjournal.org/archives/2015/05/an-al-qaeda-front-group-in-syria.php)

[141] Thomas Joscelyn. "An al Qaeda Front Group in Syria," *Long War Journal*, May 2, 2015. (http://www.longwarjournal.org/archives/2015/05/an-al-qaeda-front-group-in-syria.php)

David Andrew Weinberg   November 17, 2015

of private donations to al-Qaeda linked terrorists in Syria.[142] Unlike Qatar, Kuwait at least has pressed criminal charges since then against several suspected terror financiers, although its efforts to do so have been remarkably inconsistent.

Khorasan cell leader Muhsin al-Fadhli, who also at one point directed al-Qaeda's core financial pipeline from the Gulf to South Asia by means of Iran, was once arrested and convicted in Kuwait of funding al-Qaeda attacks, including against the U.S.S. Cole.[143] However, a Kuwaiti appeals court let him out of prison, reportedly on the absurd grounds that his crimes merely were not committed inside Kuwait.[144] He promptly fled the country after being released, and the lawyer who successfully defended al-Fadhli went on to become a member of parliament.[145]

Until 2008, Kuwait reportedly obstructed an American effort at the U.N. Security Council to impose U.N. sanctions against three prominent Kuwaiti preachers whom the U.S. believed "continue[d] to fundraise and promote terrorism and attacks on Coalition Forces in Iraq and Afghanistan."[146] The three were already under U.S. sanctions since 2006 on charges of being senior al-Qaeda financial facilitators, including for al-Qaeda in Iraq.[147]

One of those Kuwaitis, Hamid Abdullah al-Ali, was later permitted to travel to Qatar in 2013, where he reportedly praised Syrian jihadists in a sermon at Qatar's state-controlled Grand Mosque.[148] According to Treasury, he also worked closely with a Qatari now under U.S. and U.N. sanctions to fund al-Qaeda's Nusra Front.[149] Another of the three Kuwaiti clerics, Mubarak al-Bathali, was just sentenced to three years in jail by Kuwait's top court, but the charges were for Twitter posts deemed hateful toward Shi'ite Islam, not for his alleged funding of al-Qaeda.[150]

As I revealed in January 2014, Kuwait's amir swore in a new minister in charge of the country's Justice Ministry and Islamic Affairs Ministry who had purportedly endorsed three different

---

[142] U.S. Treasury Department, "Remarks of Under Secretary for Terrorism and Financial Intelligence David Cohen before the Center for a New American Security on 'Confronting New Threats in Terrorist Financing,'" March 4, 2014. (http://www.treasury.gov/press-center/press-releases/Pages/jl2308.aspx); Karen DeYoung, "Kuwait, an Ally on Syria, is also the Leading Funder of Extremist Rebels." Washington Post, April 25, 2014. (https://www.washingtonpost.com/world/national-security/kuwait-top-ally-on-syria-is-also-the-leading-funder-of-extremist-rebels/2014/04/25/10142b9a-ca48-11e3-a75e-463587891b57_story.html)
[143] "الكويت في للقاعدة بانتمائهم مشتبهين أربعة تبرئة" al-Jazeera (Qatar), April 29, 2004. (http://goo.gl/bcKqC9)
[144] "الكويت في للقاعدة بانتمائهم مشتبهين أربعة تبرئة" al-Jazeera (Qatar), April 29, 2004. (http://goo.gl/bcKqC9)
[145] "Al-Qaeda Suspects in Kuwait Trial Plead Not Guilty," Arab News (Saudi Arabia), December 17, 2002. (http://www.arabnews.com/node/226749)
[146] "Evaluation of Terrorist Facilitators / Inciters Designations in 1267 Committee," Wikileaks, February 13, 2007. (https://wikileaks.org/plusd/cables/07USUNNEWYORK129_a.html); "Terror Finance: Another Run at the MFA on Terrorist Facilitators and RIHS," Wikileaks, May 28, 2007. (https://www.wikileaks.org/plusd/cables/07KUWAIT832_a.html)
[147] U.S. Treasury Department, "Treasury Designations Target Terrorist Facilitators," December 7, 2006. (http://www.treasury.gov/press-center/press-releases/Pages/hp191.aspx)
[148] Andrew Gilligan, "The 'Club Med for Terrorists'," The Telegraph (UK), September 27, 2014. (http://www.telegraph.co.uk/news/worldnews/middleeast/qatar/11125897/The-Club-Med-for-terrorists.html)
[149] U.S. Treasury Department, "U.S. Designates Financial Supporters of Al-Qaida and Al-Nusrah Front," August 5, 2014. (http://www.treasury.gov/press-center/press-releases/Pages/jl0143.aspx)
[150] Mubarak al-Abdullah, "«التمييز» حبس البذالي 3 سنوات بسبب «تغريدة»" al-Qabas (Kuwait), November 9, 2015. (http://www.alqabas.com.kw/Articles.aspx?ArticleID=1105397&CatID=102)

David Andrew Weinberg   November 17, 2015

fundraising networks that were supporting violent extremists in Syria.[151] The Treasury Department called out Nayef al-Ajmi's ministerial appointment as "a step in the wrong direction" and revealed that one of those networks was implicated in funding al-Qaeda.[152] After a protracted public battle between the two governments, that minister stepped down.

Two individuals from his tribe have even been sanctioned by the United States and the U.N. on terror finance charges: Hajjaj and Shafi al-Ajmi. Hajjaj has complained that his bank accounts were closed,[153] and both men were briefly questioned by Kuwaiti authorities after international sanctions were imposed.[154] However, they were released within a matter of hours and do not appear to have been subject to criminal proceedings since then.

The Ajmis' tribe is not the only one in Kuwait that appears to have been exploited for terrorist fundraising.[155] An individual named Abdulrahman Khalaf al-Anizi was sanctioned last year by the U.S. and the U.N. at the same time as Hajjaj and Shafi. The U.S. called him an IS financial facilitator who had directed funds from Kuwait for terrorists since 2008, including through al-Qaeda's Iran-based financial pipeline overseen by al-Fadhli.[156] Kuwaiti authorities convicted five men this past month of funding terror who were charged with raising $1.3 million for the Islamic State[157] as part of their work for two fundraising campaigns,[158] one of which was evidently targeted at members of Anizi's tribe.[159] According to press reports, two of those defendants transferred funds to SDGT Abdulrahman al-Anizi in Raqqa, including in person.[160]

According to press reports, members of another local fundraising network known as Ansar al-Sham have also been subject to Kuwaiti legal proceedings on charges of financing the Islamic State.[161] What is puzzling is that by all appearances, this campaign primarily expressed support for

[151] David Andrew Weinberg, "New Kuwaiti Justice Minister has Deep Extremist Ties," *National Interest*, January 16, 2014. (http://nationalinterest.org/commentary/new-kuwaiti-justice-minister-has-deep-extremist-ties-9719)

[152] U.S. Treasury Department, "Remarks of Under Secretary for Terrorism and Financial Intelligence David Cohen before the Center for a New American Security on 'Confronting New Threats in Terrorist Financing,'" March 4, 2014. (http://www.treasury.gov/press-center/press-releases/Pages/jl2308.aspx)

[153] @Hajaj_Alajmi. "السوري الشعب بخدمة القيام شرف مُنعت لأني متضايق ولكني البنكية؛ حساباتي وأغلقوا العمل من فصلت لأني أتضايق لم ومساعدته." *Twitter*. October 2, 2015. (https://twitter.com/Hajaj_Alajmi/status/650094562216534018)

[154] "Kuwait Detains Muslim Cleric Suspected of Funding Militants; Security Source," *Reuters*, August 20, 2014. (http://www.reuters.com/article/2014/08/20/us-syria-crisis-kuwait-cleric-idUSKBN0GK25Q20140820)

[155] Elizabeth Dickinson, "Kuwait 'the Back Office of Logistical Support' for Syria's Rebels," *The National (UAE)*, February 5, 2013. (http://www.thenational.ae/news/world/middle-east/kuwait-the-back-office-of-logistical-support-for-syrias-rebels#full)

[156] U.S. Treasury Department, "Treasury Designates Three Key Supporters of Terrorists in Syria and Iraq," August 6, 2014. (http://www.treasury.gov/press-center/press-releases/Pages/jl2605.aspx)

[157] "Kuwait Court Jails Five over Daesh Fundraising," *Gulf News (UAE)*. November 2, 2015. (http://gulfnews.com/news/gulf/kuwait/kuwait-court-jails-five-over-daesh-fundraising-1.1611852)

[158] Hussein Ali al-Abdullah, "الخيرية الحملات من «داعش» موّلوا متهمين 5 لـ سجناً سنوات 10" *al-Jarida (Kuwait)*, November 3, 2015. (http://goo.gl/1AbiUU)

[159] Ahmad Hani al-Qabas, "السوري الشعب لنصرة التبرعات جمع حملة تنظم عنزة قبيلة" *al-Watan (Kuwait)*, August 3, 2013. (http://alwatan.kuwait.tt/articledetails.aspx?id=295398&yearquarter=20133)

[160] Hussein Ali al-Abdullah, "الخيرية الحملات من «داعش» موّلوا متهمين 5 لـ سجناً سنوات 10" *al-Jarida (Kuwait)*, November 3, 2015. (http://goo.gl/1AbiUU)

[161] "سنة 15 وآخرين الكويتي طلحة أبو وحبس داعش لوالي عاماً 20 السجن" *al-Watan (Kuwait)*, August 31, 2015. (http://alwatan.kuwait.tt/articledetails.aspx?id=443935)

David Andrew Weinberg   November 17, 2015

the Nusra Front rather than IS,[162] which raises the question of whether or not Kuwaiti authorities somehow deem fundraising for al-Qaeda as a less criminal act than supporting IS.

Finally, the United States imposed terror finance sanctions against a different Kuwaiti named Hamid Hamad al-Ali in August 2014, charging that he "traveled to Syria to deliver funds" to the Nusra Front and "referred to himself as an 'al-Qaida commando'."[163] He was simultaneously sanctioned by the U.N., which stated that he also acted as a "financier, recruiter and facilitator for Islamic State in Iraq and the Levant" and was still "Kuwait-based."[164] While I have seen no indication criminal charges have been pursued against al-Ali in Kuwait, it was reported this April he was reinstated as a mosque preacher by Kuwait's minister of justice and Islamic affairs.[165]

Saudi Arabia:

Saudi Arabia has made some noteworthy improvements in the fight against terror finance since 9/11, but that was from a remarkably low baseline. In 2009, after the bulk of those improvements had been made, a memo signed by then-Secretary of State Hillary Clinton still concluded that "donors in Saudi Arabia constitute the most significant source of funding to Sunni terrorist groups worldwide" and that Hamas, al-Qaeda, the Taliban, and Lashkar-e-Taiba "probably raise millions of dollars annually from Saudi sources."[166] The U.S. praised Saudi Arabia this year for imposing sanctions on the Pakistan branch of a Salafist charity called the Revival of Islamic Heritage Society.[167] However, Riyadh has not taken similar steps against the group's Kuwait City headquarters, which is under U.S. sanctions on charges of funding al-Qaeda, nor has the kingdom pressed charges against prominent clerics who fundraised for RIHS on Saudi TV.[168]

Worryingly, Saudi Arabia has also chosen to play host to several Yemenis under U.S. terror finance sanctions. This comes in the midst of the recent war in Yemen, where Saudi-led jetfighters have established full air superiority but have not dropped a single bomb against al-Qaeda fighters operating in the open during any of the coalition's round-the-clock airstrikes.[169]

---

[162] "Fundraising Campaign in Kuwait for Designated Terrorist Group Jabhat al-Nusra Using Facebook, Twitter, Skype, YouTube," *MEMRI Cyber & Jihad Lab*, May 17, 2014. (http://cjlab.memri.org/lab-projects/tracking-jihadi-terrorist-use-of-social-media/fundraising-campaign-in-kuwait-for-designated-terrorist-group-jabhat-al-nusra-using-facebook-twitter-skype-youtube/)
[163] U.S. Treasury Department, "Treasury Designates Additional Supporters of the Al-Nusrah Front and Al-Qaida," August 22, 2014. (http://www.treasury.gov/press-center/press-releases/Pages/jl2613.aspx)
[164] U.N. Security Council, "Consolidated United Nations Security Council Sanctions List," November 12, 2014. (https://www.un.org/sc/suborg/sites/www.un.org.sc.suborg/files/consolidated.htm)
[165] Turki al-Maghames, "العدساني لمسجد إماماً...مجتدأ العلي حامد" *al-Rai (Kuwait)*, April 21, 2015. (http://www.alraimedia.com/ar/article/last/2015/04/21/584215/nr/kuwait)
[166] "Terrorist Finance: Action Request for Senior Level Engagement on Terrorism Finance," *Wikileaks*, December 30, 2009. (https://wikileaks.org/plusd/cables/09STATE131801_a.html)
[167] U.S. Treasury Department, "The U.S. and Saudi Arabia Take Joint Action Against Terrorist Financing Entity Attempting to Evade U.S. and UN Sanctions and Violate Saudi Laws," April 7, 2015. (http://www.treasury.gov/press-center/press-releases/Pages/jl10019.aspx)
[168] David Andrew Weinberg, "Saudi Steps on Terror Finance Fall Short," *FDD Policy Brief*, April 16, 2015. (http://www.defenddemocracy.org/media-hit/david-weinberg-saudi-steps-on-terror-finance-fall-short/)
[169] David B. Ottaway, "Saudi Arabia's 'Terrorist' Allies in Yemen," *Wilson Center Viewpoints*, no. 81, August 2015. (https://www.wilsoncenter.org/sites/default/files/saudi_arabias_terrorist_allies_in_yemen.pdf)

David Andrew Weinberg   November 17, 2015

Abdulmajeed al-Zindani is a onetime mentor to Osama Bin Laden whom the U.S. sanctioned on charges of recruiting and purchasing weapons for al-Qaeda in 2004.[170] This year he has been photographed repeatedly around Saudi Arabia, throwing a lavish wedding for his son[171] and visiting with prominent clerics, allegedly even including the kingdom's state-appointed Grand Mufti.[172] Zindani's presence in the kingdom would appear to be a violation of the travel ban imposed by the United Nations when it also imposed terror finance sanctions on him in 2004.[173]

Also spotted this year in Riyadh has been Abdulwahab al-Humayqani, a Yemeni under U.S. terror finance sanctions since 2013.[174] That year, the U.S. stated that he used his Yemen-based charity to fund al-Qaeda and reportedly "served as the acting AQAP amir" in Yemen's province of al-Bayda".[175] Thanks to his status as part of the Riyadh delegation to Yemeni ceasefire talks in Geneva, Humayqani was photographed shaking hands this summer with U.N. Secretary General Ban Ki-Moon and has been interviewed widely on regional media.[176]

Saudi Arabia's draconian Interior Ministry issued the country's first formal list of terrorist groups last year, and it was a big disappointment. It criminalized as terrorism "the promotion of atheistic thinking," protest "demonstrations," "collective statements," or "communicating with another country" if any of these acts could be perceived as undermining national unity.[177] Like the UAE's 2014 terror list, which was criticized for including several non-violent Islamic groups, Saudi Arabia's list outlawed the Muslim Brotherhood while excluding a range of Palestinian terror groups that target Israeli civilians, such as Hamas, Lebanese Hezbollah, Palestinian Islamic Jihad, and the Popular Front for the Liberation of Palestine, to name just a few.

Turkey:

In Recep Tayyip Erdoğan's haste to undermine Syria's Assad regime, Turkey allowed its southern border to become a recklessly under-regulated frontier for the flow of funding, weapons,

---

[170] U.S. Treasury Department, "United States Designates bin Laden Loyalist," February 24, 2004. (http://www.treasury.gov/press-center/press-releases/Pages/js1190.aspx)

[171] "الفضيحة!" "الزنداني بـ الزنداني عبدالمجيد الشيخ ابن زواج بصفون تويتر موقع رواد" *al-Bawaba (Jordan),* October 8, 2015. (http://goo.gl/dXTf1Q)

[172] David Andrew Weinberg, "UN Official Reportedly Meets with Iraqi on al Qaeda Sanctions List," *Long War Journal,* October 30, 2015. (http://www.longwarjournal.org/archives/2015/10/un-official-reportedly-meets-with-iraqi-on-al-qaeda-sanctions-list.php)

[173] U.N. Security Council, "Consolidated United Nations Security Council Sanctions List," November 12, 2014. (https://www.un.org/sc/suborg/sites/www.un.org.sc.suborg/files/consolidated.htm)

[174] Al Jazeera Mubasher, "تعز في الجمهوري للقصر ترحف اليمنية المقاومة .. تفاعلية نافذة" *YouTube,* August 15, 2015. (https://www.youtube.com/watch?v=UVWw0t9hQ6s&feature=youtu.be&t=4m40s)

[175] U.S. Treasury Department, "Treasury Designates Al-Qa'ida Supporters in Qatar and Yemen," December 18, 2013. (http://www.treasury.gov/press-center/press-releases/Pages/jl2249.aspx)

[176] David Andrew Weinberg, "Ban Ki-Moon Shakes Hands with Alleged al Qaeda Emir," *Long War Journal,* June 23, 2015. (http://www.longwarjournal.org/archives/2015/06/ban-ki-moon-shakes-hands-with-alleged-al-qaeda-emir.php)

[177] "Full text of Saudi Interior Ministry statement designating terrorist organizations," *Asharq al-Awsat (UK),* March 8, 2014. (http://english.aawsat.com/2014/03/article55329804/full-text-of-saudi-interior-ministry-statement-announcing-terrorist-list)

David Andrew Weinberg   November 17, 2015

ammunition, and recruits to al-Qaeda and IS.[178] Last year, oil sales became IS's largest source of income, and smuggling through Turkey seemed to be a primary destination for such shipments as well as for stolen antiquities.[179] At times Turkish border guards allegedly looked the other way, and while Ankara's efforts may have gotten more serious in this regard, some believe it "created a monster" it no longer can control.[180] And according to Britain's *The Independent*, "Turkish officials admit giving logistical and intelligence support to the command headquarters" in Idlib of the Army of Conquest, and "although they deny giving direct help to Al-Nusra, they acknowledge that the group would be beneficiaries" as a member of the Army.[181]

Turkey's recent role as a *mujahideen* gateway for Syria and Iraq should come as little surprise to those who followed Ankara's role involving several types of illicit finance over the last decade.

Turkey's state-owned Halkbank reportedly helped state sponsor of terrorism Iran circumvent the spirit of international sanctions by purchasing billions of dollars worth of Iranian natural gas and enabling Iranians to move the proceeds in the form of gold.[182] Iranian-Azeri businessman Reza Zerrab was accused of using exorbitant gifts and personal connections to members of Turkey's cabinet in order to facilitate "irregular money transactions, mostly from Iran, that total some 87 billion euros," moving "almost a metric ton of gold to Iran every day for 1 ½ years."[183]

Turkish press reports alleged Saudi businessman Yasin al-Qadi visited the country illegally four times between February and October 2012 without a passport or visa.[184] Qadi was supposed to be under a U.N. travel ban until the U.N. terror finance sanctions on him were lifted that October.[185]

---

[178] Jonathan Schanzer and Merve Tahiroglu, *Bordering on Terrorism: Turkey's Syria Policy and the Rise of the Islamic State*, FDD Press, November 2014.
(http://www.defenddemocracy.org/content/uploads/publications/bordering-on-terrorism.pdf)
[179] U.S. Treasury Department, "Remarks of Under Secretary for Terrorism and Financial Intelligence David S. Cohen at The Carnegie Endowment For International Peace, 'Attacking ISIL's Financial Foundation,'" October 23, 2014; (http://www.treasury.gov/press-center/press-releases/Pages/jl2672.aspx); Mike Giglio and Munzer al-Awad, "Inside the Underground Trade to Sell off Syria's History," *BuzzFeed News*, July 30, 2015.
(http://www.buzzfeed.com/mikegiglio/the-trade-in-stolen-syrian-artifacts#.lllv689nN)
[180] Mike Giglio, "This is How ISIS Smuggles Oil," *BuzzFeed News*, November 3, 2014.
(http://www.buzzfeed.com/mikegiglio/this-is-how-isis-smuggles-oil#.ewQDa8xvb); Yaroslav Trofimov, "Porous Syria-Turkey Border Poses Challenge in Fight against Islamic State: Fighters, Oil, and Military Supplies Flow across Border," *Wall Street Journal*, February 19, 2015. (http://www.wsj.com/articles/porous-syria-turkey-border-poses-challenge-in-fight-against-islamic-state-1424334057)
[181] Kim Sengupta, "Turkey and Saudi Arabia Alarm the West by Backing Islamist Extremists the Americans had Bombed in Syria." *The Independent (UK)*, May 13, 2015. (http://www.independent.co.uk/news/world/middle-east/syria-crisis-turkey-and-saudi-arabia-shock-western-countries-by-supporting-anti-assad-jihadists-10242747.html)
[182] Jonathan Schanzer and Mark Dubowitz. "Iran's Turkish Gold Rush." *Foreign Policy*, December 26, 2013. (http://foreignpolicy.com/2013/12/26/irans-turkish-gold-rush/)
[183] Mehul Srivastava, "Turkey Crisis Puts Jailed Millionaire at Heart of Gold Trail," *Bloomberg*, January 29, 2014. (http://www.bloomberg.com/news/articles/2014-01-29/turkey-scandal-places-jailed-millionaire-at-center-of-gold-trail); "87 Billion Euros in Suspicious Transfers from Iran," *Today's Zaman (Turkey)*, December 17, 2013. (http://www.todayszaman.com/diplomacy_87-billion-euros-in-suspicious-transfers-from-iran_334277.html)
[184] Jonathan Schanzer. *Terrorism Finance in Turkey: A Growing Concern*, FDD Press. February 2014. p. 12. (http://www.defenddemocracy.org/content/uploads/documents/Schanzer_Turkey_Final_Report_3_smaller.pdf)
[185] U.N. Security Council, "Security Council Al-Qaida Sanctions Committee Deletes Entry of Yasin Abdullah Ezzedine Qadi from its List." October 5, 2012. (http://www.un.org/press/en/2012/sc10785.doc.htm)

David Andrew Weinberg   November 17, 2015

While there, he allegedly had a state escort and met Erdoğan, Erdoğan's son, and Turkey's intelligence chief.[186]

~~Along with Qatar, Turkey has also been accused in press reports of channeling up to several hundred million dollars~~ in state funds to the U.S.-designated Foreign Terrorist Organization Hamas ~~or entities under its control in the Gaza Strip.[187]~~

Hamas's Regional Financial Network:

The U.S. Treasury Department imposed sanctions this September on four individuals and one company as "key players in Hamas's international fundraising operational network."[188] Although Treasury did not explicitly say so, the reported activities of these entities reflect quite negatively on Riyadh, Doha, and Ankara.

The most well-known of these individuals was Salah al-Arouri, a member of Hamas's politburo. The September sanctions represented the first time the U.S. government publicly confirmed that Arouri had used his base in Turkey to "oversee[] the distribution of Hamas finances" and "direct[] military operations in the West Bank."[189]

~~The U.S. also sanctioned Mahir Salah, known as Abu Aref, who it said "has led the Hamas Finance Committee in Saudi Arabia, the largest center of Hamas's financial activity."[190] It added that Salah managed front companies and laundered money for the group, charging that he "has overseen the transfer of tens of millions of dollars from Iran to Saudi Arabia," and ultimately on to Hamas's military wing in Gaza.[191]~~

Arabic news reports suggest that Mahir Salah also played a critical role supervising Hamas's regional financial network from Jeddah, including major operations not just in Saudi Arabia but

[186] "Erdoğan defends Saudi Arabia after Hajj disaster, raises eyebrows." *Today's Zaman (Turkey)*, September 27, 2015. (http://www.todayszaman.com/anasayfa_erdogan-defends-saudi-arabia-after-hajj-disaster-raises-eyebrows_400005.html)
[187] Saed Bannoura, "Turkey to Grant Hamas $300 Million," *International Middle East Media Center (PA)*, December 3, 2013. (http://www.imemc.org/article/62607); Nidal al-Mughrabi, Hamas Quietly Quits Syria as Violence Continues." *Reuters*, January 27, 2012. (http://www.reuters.com/article/2012/01/27/us-syria-hamas-idUSTRE80Q0QS20120127#QR8pXWeJoZAq1uIL.97)
[188] U.S. Treasury Department, "Treasury Sanctions Major Hamas Leaders, Financial Facilitators and a Front Company," September 10, 2015. (http://www.treasury.gov/press-center/press-releases/Pages/jl0159.aspx)
[189] U.S. Treasury Department, "Treasury Sanctions Major Hamas Leaders, Financial Facilitators and a Front Company," September 10, 2015. (http://www.treasury.gov/press-center/press-releases/Pages/jl0159.aspx)
[190] U.S. Treasury Department, "Treasury Sanctions Major Hamas Leaders, Financial Facilitators and a Front Company," September 10, 2015. (http://www.treasury.gov/press-center/press-releases/Pages/jl0159.aspx)
[191] U.S. Treasury Department, "Treasury Sanctions Major Hamas Leaders, Financial Facilitators and a Front Company," September 10, 2015. (http://www.treasury.gov/press-center/press-releases/Pages/jl0159.aspx)

David Andrew Weinberg   November 17, 2015

also in Qatar,[192] Turkey,[193] Egypt,[194] and Sudan[195] – often in the millions or tens of millions of dollars. What the Treasury Department also did not mention is that Saudi Arabia recently released him and his subordinates from prison.

Press reports suggest that Abu Aref was arrested by Saudi Arabia in December,[196] and his detention was apparently on the basis of an American request, according to the Qatari-owned news site *al-Araby al-Jadeed*.[197] However, soon afterwards Saudi Arabia's King Salman succeeded his half-brother on the throne and began to embrace Islamist hardliners, making new overtures to Hamas and other groups associated with the Muslim Brotherhood. Hamas leader Khaled Meshal was allowed to visit the kingdom for the first time in years, meeting the king and his powerful son Mohammed, among others. A main focus of the visit was to seek the release of Abu Aref and seven subordinates, a gesture allegedly granted at the end of their meeting with Prince Mohammed.[198]

Another Jeddah-based individual sanctioned by Treasury in September was Abu Ubaydah al-Agha, a Saudi citizen with familial origins in Gaza who has managed his family's Jeddah-based firm, Asyaf International.[199] The U.S. government alleged that he was "a senior Hamas financial officer involved in investment, funding, and money transfers for Hamas in Saudi Arabia" and that Asyaf was "a front company" used to assist the group with money transfers, investments, and financial services since at least 2005.[200]

It seems Abu Ubaydah's late father Khairy Hafiz al-Agha may have been an unindicted coconspirator in the Hamas finance case brought by U.S. officials against the Holy Land Foundation.[201] A Saudi-based Khairy H. al-Agha allegedly helped run a company that sent $1.3 million to HLF's leaders and received $250,000 from them between 1988 and 1991.[202] When al-

[192] "حماس" تحول أنشطتها المالية من السعودية إلى قطر وتركيا" *al-Seyassah (Kuwait)*, April 7, 2014. (http://goo.gl/4vc3Zl);
"الأخرى تلو واحدة تتكشف "حماس" قيادات صفوف في الفساد قضايا" *al-Seyassah (Kuwait)*, January 8, 2013.
[193] "وتركيا استياء داخل أوساط رسمية دعم من تركية أردوغان "ل"حماس على الصعيدين السياسى والمالي" *al-Seyassah (Kuwait)*, June 28, 2013.
[194] ""السابع اليوم"لـ ومصادر .. الأموال غسيل بتهمة لحماس المسئول المالى تعتقل السعودية" *al-Youm al-Sabi' (Egypt)*, April 19, 2015. (http://goo.gl/cHPhK4); "أبوعارف".. مصر في حماس حركة أموال يدير الذي للغامض الكاملة القصة" *ElMogaz (Egypt)*, December 21, 2013. (http://www.elmogaz.com/node/119383)
[195] "أبوعارف".. مصر في حماس حركة أموال يدير الذي للغامض الكاملة القصة" *ElMogaz (Egypt)*, December 21, 2013. (http://www.elmogaz.com/node/119383)
[196] ""السابع اليوم"لـ ومصادر .. الأموال غسيل بتهمة لحماس المسئول المالى تعتقل السعودية" *al-Youm al-Sabi' (Egypt)*, April 19, 2015. (http://goo.gl/cHPhK4); "مشعل بإطلاق ينجح معتقلي حماس في السعودية" *Palestine Press News Agency (PA)*, July 17, 2015. (http://palpress.co.uk/arabic/?Action=Details&ID=111064)
[197] "مشعل زيارة بعد "حماس" معتقلي تطلق السعودية" *al-Araby al-Jadeed (UK)*, July 18, 2015. (http://goo.gl/nzlq2U)
[198] Ali Hashem, "Hamas Caught between Tehran and Riyadh," *Al-Monitor*, August 23, 2015. (http://www.al-monitor.com/pulse/originals/2015/08/iran-hamas-ties-saudi-arabia.html); Muhammad Hassan Amer, "محمود الزهار"؛ زيارة "مشعل" للرياض كسرت جمود العلاقات" *El Watan News (Egypt)*, July 20, 2015. (http://www.elwatannews.com/news/details/772297)
[199] U.S. Treasury Department, "Treasury Sanctions Major Hamas Leaders, Financial Facilitators and a Front Company," September 10, 2015. (http://www.treasury.gov/press-center/press-releases/Pages/jl0159.aspx)
[200] U.S. Treasury Department, "Treasury Sanctions Major Hamas Leaders, Financial Facilitators and a Front Company," September 10, 2015. (http://www.treasury.gov/press-center/press-releases/Pages/jl0159.aspx)
[201] U.S. District Court for the Northern District of Texas, "List of Unindicted Co-Conspirators and/or Joint Volunteers," May 29, 2007. (http://www.investigativeproject.org/documents/case_docs/423.pdf)
[202] U.S. District Court for the Northern District of Texas, "Payments to K&A Trading," Exhibit List: USA v. Holy Land Foundation for Relief and Development, September 29, 2008. (http://coop.txnd.uscourts.gov/judges/hlf2/09-

David Andrew Weinberg   November 17, 2015

Agha died in 2014, a reception was held in Qatar attended by Meshal himself, who said they had a "personal relationship" since the 1980s "in supporting the Gaza Strip."[203]

According to the *Christian Science Monitor*, Qatar briefly detained "two Hamas financiers" in late December 2014, a moment when Doha was under pressure from Riyadh to crack down on Hamas and other Brotherhood-linked groups; Saudi Arabia's King Abdullah passed away in January, and the detainees were swiftly released.[204]

Sitting with Meshal at the wake for Khairy al-Agha was Mohammed al-Qawasmi, whom the Kuwaiti daily *al-Seyassah* described in January as a Hamas financial officer recently detained by Doha.[205] Yet video footage from later this year shows Qawasmi speaking at another event in Qatar alongside Meshal.[206] Notably, he was allowed to co-host a show promoting a Gaza fundraiser on state-controlled Qatari TV just last summer[207] despite having long been identified as a local member of Hamas.[208]

Like Qawasmi, Zahir al-Jabareen has been described as a Hamas official who reportedly worked from Qatar to channel funding from the Gulf into the West Bank for Hamas.[209] Press reports suggest that he has since been spotted in Turkey, serving as a deputy to Arouri as part of a bureau in Turkey that trains new Hamas recruits.[210] Also spending time in Qatar has been Maher Ubeid, a member of Hamas's politburo who reportedly was put in charge of laundering tens of millions

29-08/Payments%20to%20K%20Agha%20KA%20Trading.pdf); U.S. District Court for the Northern District of Texas, "Payments to K&A Marzook," Exhibit List: USA v. Holy Land Foundation for Relief and Development, September 29, 2008. (http://coop.txnd.uscourts.gov/judges/hlf2/09-29-08/KA%20Marzook.pdf); "Holy Land Evidence Establishes Hamas Link" *IPT News*, September 29, 2008. (http://www.investigativeproject.org/781/holy-land-evidence-establishes-hamas-link#); *United States of America v. Mohammad El-Mezain, et al*, Revised December 27, 2011 in the United States Court of Appeals for the Fifth Circuit, No. 09-10560, (Appeal from the United States District Court for the Northern District of Texas, December 7, 2011). (http://federalevidence.com/pdf/United%20States%20v.%20El-Mezain,%20No.%202009-10560%20(5th%20Cir.%20Dec.%207,%202011).pdf)

[203] "الأغا حافظ خيري المرحوم العائلة عميد عزاء بيت صور –الدوحة" *El-Agha Family Tree website*, June 3, 2014. (http://elagha.net/?do=2&id=10345)

[204] Taylor Luck, "In Hamas Leader's Exit from Qatar, Signs of Growing Saudi-Egyptian Influence," *Christian Science Monitor*, January 26, 2015. (http://www.csmonitor.com/World/Middle-East/2015/0126/In-Hamas-leader-s-exit-from-Qatar-signs-of-growing-Saudi-Egyptian-influence)

[205] "المالية كوادرها أحد قطر اعتقال بعد "حماس" داخل حادة انتقادات يواجه مشعل" *al-Seyassah (Kuwait)*. January 28, 2015. (http://goo.gl/TSTm9q)

[206] "الأغا زكريا يحيى ريما .أ وخطوبة إشهار حفل –الدوحة" *El-Agha Family Tree website*, August 31, 2015. "الأغا يحيى ريما .أ وخطوبة إشهار حفل حمدة وأبو الأغا عائلة جامعة" (http://elagha.net/print.php?id=11789); Sofian Elagha, *YouTube*, August 30, 2015. (https://www.youtube.com/watch?v=5FNjP9JQM-M)

[207] Alrayyan TV, "المختصر برنامج - الحلقة الحاديه و الاربعون - 06-08-2014" *YouTube*, August 7, 2014. (https://youtu.be/mAFcUhneLHE?t=34m44s)

[208] Abdulhakim Ahmein, "والعراق لفلسطين دعما قطر في شعبية مسيرة" *al-Jazeera (Qatar)*, March 29, 2007. (http://goo.gl/dhTtw3)

[209] "مصر في حماس حركة أموال يدير الذي للغامض الكاملة القصة ..أبو عارف" *ElMogaz (Egypt)*, December 21, 2013. (http://www.elmogaz.com/node/119383)

[210] Amos Harel, "Stopping the Nuclear Deal won't Halt the Regional Funding of Terror," *Ha'aretz (Israel)*, August 9, 2015. (http://www.haaretz.com/israel-news/.premium-1.670067); Alex Fishman, "Forced from Damascus, Hamas Establishing Itself in Turkey," *Ynet News (Israel)*, February 25, 2015. (http://www.ynetnews.com/articles/0,7340,L-4630331,00.html)

David Andrew Weinberg November 17, 2015

of euros from Turkish territory, including allegedly from the Turkish state, to Hamas's military and political wings in Gaza.[211]

Coming back full circle to the challenge of kidnapping for ransom by terrorist groups, it is important to recognize that several key operatives in Hamas's regional financial empire gained their freedom as part of the Gilad Shalit prisoner exchange, whereby over a thousand Palestinian and Israeli-Arab prisoners were released in an arrangement extracted by Hamas for a single captive Israeli soldier.

Arouri was released from Israeli prison some years before the Shalit deal, and his deputy Jabireen was freed as part of the swap. So were several others accused by Israel or in press reports since then of significant financial activities on behalf of Hamas via either Turkey or Qatar. They include Hussam Badran,[212] Talal Shareem,[213] Hisham Hijazi,[214] and Jibril Juneid.[215]

It would seem that these developments offer a cautionary tale as to one possible risk of exchanging hostages for ransom or other concessions to terrorists.

There would seem to be a similar unfortunate postscript to the case of the kidnapped Israeli soldier whose wife I watched the late Rep. Lantos try to console and reassure at a 2007 event in this very building. The next year, when Hezbollah returned that soldier's lifeless body and the body of his colleague, it was in a trade for the bodies of 199 militants taken by Israel as well as in exchange for five living prisoners being held in Israeli jails.

One of those returnees, Samir Kuntar, had slaughtered five members of an Israeli family, including two young children, in a notoriously gruesome 1979 attack. This September, the U.S. indicated that Kuntar has joined Hezbollah, "emerg[ing] as one of the group's most visible and popular spokesmen" and "play[ing] an operational role, with the assistance of Iran and Syria, in building up Hizballah's terrorist infrastructure in the Golan Heights."[216]

Policy Recommendations on Combating Private Donations to Terrorists:

The United States needs a greater range of policy options to escalate the dispute when these allies refuse to take action against known financiers of groups linked to al-Qaeda. There are several key

[211] "غزة على سيطرتها لتعزيز "حماس"الـتركيا من يورو مليون 40" *Palestine Press News Agency (PA)*. November 6, 2012. (http://www.palpress.co.uk/arabic/?Action=Details&ID=65344); "استياء أوساط داخل رسمية من تركية دعم أردوغان اللامحدود"; "حماس"ال على الصعيدين السياسي المالي"و *al-Seyassah (Kuwait)*. June 28. 2013.

[212] Yoav Zitun, "Shin Bet Arrests 40 Hamas Members in Nablus," *Ynet News* (Israel), July 1, 2015. (http://www.ynetnews.com/articles/0,7340,L-4674956,00.html); "Hamas Terrorist Assets Revealed in Hebron," *Israel Defense Forces*, accessed July 6, 2015. (http://www.idf.il/1153-18193-en/Dover.aspx)

[213] Yonah Jeremy Bob, "Shin Bet Busts Palestinian Footballer For Meeting With Hamas Terrorist In Qatar," *Jerusalem Post* (Israel), June 11, 2014. (http://www.jpost.com/Sports/Palestinian-soccer-player-admits-to-meeting-with-Hamas-operative-while-in-Qatar-356003)

[214] "Security Forces Capture Hamas Terrorist," *Israel Defense Forces*, March 6. 2013. (http://www.idf.il/1283-19091-EN/Dover.aspx)

[215] "الحركة اموال من دولار مليون 12 بسرقة مشعل خالد تتهم حماس" *Palestine News Network (PA)*, October 7, 2012. (http://www.shfanews.net/index.php/2012-02-15-08-44-39/11664-i)

[216] U.S. State Department, "Terrorist Designation of Samir Kuntar," September 8, 2015. (http://www.state.gov/r/pa/prs/ps/2015/09/246687.htm)

David Andrew Weinberg   November 17, 2015

steps the U.S. government and Congress in particular can take to avoid the risk of America's Specially Designated Global Terrorist list being a mere toothless piece of paper:

1. Encourage Administration Officials to Speak Out. The Treasury Department gets it: these countries are not reliable partners in the fight against private terror finance. But there is more that can be done to boost Treasury's hand at eliciting cooperation from these states. Congress can play a much-needed role sensitizing other parts of the executive branch to the severity of this problem and to the risk that it could pose to America's Mideast alliances. Treasury's message would be far more compelling in regional capitals if it was being consistently echoed by the White House, State Department (including but not limited to Embassy Doha), Defense Department (particularly CENTCOM), Homeland Security, Justice, Commerce, and intelligence agencies. The White House should also be encouraged to give Treasury a free hand to go public with its concerns, as it did in 2014 by calling out Qatar and Kuwait for bad behavior.

2. Threaten to Take Independent Action. In cases where Washington is truly convinced of its intelligence that a resident in one of these countries is enjoying legal impunity for acts of terror finance, there are a range of independent actions that the U.S. could take to address the problem. First, it could privately threaten to seek that individual's extradition, just as we do with drug lords, illegal arms dealers, and even crooked sports officials, in hopes of pressuring the host government to file needed legal charges on its own. Second, if that does not work, the United States could call for the individual's extradition in public, shaming the host government for granting legal impunity to bad actors. Finally, the U.S. intelligence, military, and law enforcement communities could be given a green light to kill or capture the individual in the same manner that they do with other sorts of senior terrorist operatives.

3. Restrict Trade in Dual Use Items. The Export Administration Act of 1979 calls for strict licensing requirements for trade in dual-use items to countries that knowingly grant safe haven to operatives of terrorist groups, as many of these countries do, particularly in the case of Hamas. This list of goods includes items that a group like Hamas would love to get its hands on: advanced missile equipment, precursors for weapons of mass destruction, and technology for cyber warfare. Congress would be fully within its rights to warn the executive branch in letters, private meetings, or new legislation that it seeks to impose these sorts of penalties against countries such as Turkey and Qatar which have long been eager for advanced American technology but also are longtime hosts of military, financial, and political leaders for Hamas.

4. Seek to Amend the Foreign Sovereign Immunity Act. In 1996, Congress amended the Foreign Sovereign Immunity Act to let U.S. citizens sue state sponsors of terrorism in civil court for damages caused by terrorist attacks for which they bore responsibility. Congress could amend the FSIA again to extend that legal liability to governments that provide safe haven and legal impunity to terrorist operatives or financial facilitators of Foreign Terrorist Organizations with regard to acts committed by those FTOs. Unlike designated state sponsors of terror such as Iran, the negligent U.S. allies described in this testimony would be more responsive to such a threat because they have much greater exposure to the U.S. economy, and it would also concentrate the focus of the executive branch on pressing these countries to adopt more responsible behavior.

Mr. POE. Thank you, Dr. Weinberg.
Ms. Foley.

STATEMENT OF MS. DIANE FOLEY, FOUNDER, JAMES W. FOLEY LEGACY FOUNDATION INC.

Ms. FOLEY. I am Diane Foley, mother of American journalist, James Foley, who was publically executed by ISIS, as you know, in August 2014.

And I certainly want to say that our thoughts and prayers are with the people of France and who have suffered such tragic loss at the hands of ISIS.

But we too as Americans have suffered from ISIS. Our son, James, was tortured and starved by ISIS for nearly 2 years just for being an American.

Our family's ordeal was made worse by our incoherent and often ineffective hostage policy. Jim was the oldest of our five children born into a very average American middle class family.

He was well educated, holding two Master's degrees in writing and journalism. But far more importantly, he was a man of service—teaching in our inner cities in Phoenix through Teach for America and later in Chicago and Massachusetts.

He was always passionate about those without a voice, be they hostages, conflict journalists or disadvantaged children in our inner cities. In fact, his belief in human rights actually led him to become a journalist so that we Americans might hear the unheard stories of suffering in conflict zones.

In my opinion, our current American hostage policy has not changed. I am very aware that our U.S. public policy is no concessions to terrorists to include no ransom or release of prisoners.

However, our policy also states that the United States will use every appropriate resource to gain the safe return of our American citizens held hostage by terrorists.

During Jim's horrific captivity in Syria, our policy was interpreted to mean no concessions, no engagement with his captors. Since 9/11, our Government officials have often mistaken no concessions for meaning no negotiations, leading to an inconsistent and often unjust approach to the kidnapping of our citizens.

The hands of our powerful FBI were tied during the 2014 Syrian captivity of our son, Jim, and three other American citizens held by ISIS.

I am told that our strict adherence to this policy saves lives by decreasing the rate of capture of Americans. But no one has been able to show me the research behind our hostage policy.

In fact, it would seem that Americans are becoming targets at an alarming rate. I respectfully demand to see the proof that our current hostage policy is truly protecting Americans.

It did not protect Jim or Steven or Kayla or Peter. In the last 18 months, these four Americans have been killed because our policy was strictly applied, whereas five other Americans—Casey Coombs, Sam Farren, Scott Darden, Theo Curtis and Sgt. Bergdahl—who were negotiated for by us or others have returned home safely.

This inconsistent implementation of our American hostage policy is unacceptable. Additionally, I would have you gentlemen know that we were deceived as an American family.

We were told repeatedly that Jim was their highest priority—your highest priority. We trusted our Government to help him return home.

During the brief month that Jim's ISIS captors reached out to negotiate for his release, our Government refused to engaged with the ISIS captors, leaving us alone as parents to negotiate for our son's freedom.

Eighteen months after Jim's captivity our family and three other families of hostages held with Jim in Syria were threatened by Col. Mark Mitchell, member of our National Security Council, with prosecution by our Government, although there was never any precedent, if we attempted to raise a ransom to free our loved ones.

He also very clearly told us that our Government would not ask allies to help negotiate release and would never conduct any military operation to rescue them.

He made it very clear that our United States Government planned to abandon these four Americans. Thus, it became clear that Jim, Peter, Steven and Kayla were considered collateral damage and that we families were truly on our own.

I had spent much of our family's savings, quit my job as a nurse practitioner to travel monthly to Washington to beg for help for Jim, to the United Nations, countless Embassies and to Europe multiple times to speak to freed hostages, all to no avail.

While our U.S. senators reached out to us and were sympathetic, we never even heard from our United States congressman. The family—the Foley family did try to raise a ransom for Jim's relief in spite of threats of prosecution.

But because we believed in our Government to help, we started much too late and were unable to raise the money to interest ISIS. The reality is that very few families would be able to raise money actually needed to free their loved ones.

Our U.S. Government also refused to engage at a high level with our allies who also had citizens held by ISIS. At one point, there were over 20 Western hostages held together and all of them our allies.

In the spring of 2014, a freed French hostage had very specific information from ISIS to negotiate for our four American hostages and the three British ones. But our Government refused to engage with the French or U.K. to save our citizens.

The result is that all the European hostages are now home whereas our son, the other Americans and British were brutally killed.

Although we had specific information regarding the exact location of their captivity beginning in the fall of 2013, a military operation was not even attempted until July 2014 after all the Europeans were safely home.

We are sincerely grateful to the brave soldiers making that attempt but it was much too late. In our situation, our hostage policy prohibited our Government from interacting in any way with Jim's captors, prohibited even from investigating who our son's captors were.

Had our Government been allowed to engage the captors, perhaps vital intelligence about ISIS might have been gleaned. Our Government's abandonment of Jim allowed their deaths to be used as propaganda for ISIS recruitment, thus strengthening and emboldening ISIS.

It surely helped in their recruitment of other violent people who want to destroy us. As I said before, at one point there were more than 20 Western hostages held together, all of whom are citizens of our allies. All our Western allies value their citizens enough to negotiate for their freedom.

Had Jim been French, Spanish, German, Italian or Danish he would be alive today. You know, we form coalitions for war. Why did we not engage with our allies to free all the Western hostages?

I believe that much stronger coalitions with our allies are essential to deal with the shrewdness and hatred of these terrorist groups. I fear that our posture of no engagement with Jim's ISIS captors led to our underestimation of their intelligence and their deep-seated hatred for the United States and our citizens.

What if we had been shrewd enough to engage Jim's Syrian captors in the fall of 2013 to learn all we could about them instead of ignoring them? Is it ever wise to ignore enemies of freedom and justice?

You know, Jim believed in America. He believed that our Government valued him as a journalist, as a citizen. I am told he was hopeful until the very end of his 20 months of captivity.

He and our family were truly abandoned by our Government. How would you feel if one of your sons or daughters had been in Jim's predicament and had been treated similarly?

Four Americans were publicly beheaded. Where is our outrage as Americans? Is an individual American citizen no longer valuable? Why would Jim and the other Americans in Syria considered collateral damage?

If our United States of America truly wants to protect and prioritize the return of its citizens, if so I ask you esteemed Members of Congress to hold this new fusion cell accountable for the return of our American citizens and to mandate a thorough reevaluation of our current hostage policy to make sure that recent validated research is being done to ensure that our policy truly saves the lives of Americans.

Thank you for your attention. I appreciate it.

[The prepared statement of Ms. Foley follows:]

Diane M. Foley
Testimony- November 17, 2015
House Committee on Foreign Affairs
Subcommittee-Terrorism, Nonproliferation, and Trade

Dear respected members of Congress,

I am Diane Foley, the mother of American journalist James Foley, who was publicly executed by ISIS in August 2014.

First, I want to say that my thoughts and prayers are with the people of France who have suffered such tragic loss at the hands of ISIS.

We too have suffered from ISIS. Our son James was tortured and starved by ISIS for nearly 2 years, just for being an American. Our family's ordeal was made worse by our incoherent and ineffective hostage policy.

Jim was the oldest of our five children born into an average middle class American family. Jim was well educated, holding two Master's degrees, in writing and in journalism; but more importantly he was a man of service, teaching in our US inner cities of Phoenix through Teach for America, and later in Chicago and Massachusetts. He was passionate about those without a voice, be they hostages, conflict journalists or disadvantaged children in our inner cities. In fact, his belief in basic human rights led him to become a journalist, to tell us the unheard stories of the suffering in conflict zones.

Our current American hostage policy has not changed. I am very aware of our US public policy of no concessions to terrorists, to include no ransom or release of prisoners. However, our policy also states that the United States will use every appropriate resource to gain the safe return of American citizens who are held hostage by terrorists. During Jim's horrific captivity in Syria, our policy was interpreted to mean no negotiations, no engagement with his captors.

Since 9/11, our Government has often mistaken no concessions for no negotiations, leading to an inconsistent, unjust approach to the kidnapping of our citizens. The hands of our powerful FBI were tied during the 2014 Syrian captivity of our son Jim and the three other American citizens held by ISIS. I am told our strict adherence to this policy saves lives by decreasing the rate of capture of Americans; but no one has been able to show me the research behind our hostage policy. In fact, it would seem that Americans are becoming targets at an alarming rate!

I respectfully demand to see the proof that our current hostage policy is truly protecting Americans. It did not protect Jim, Steven, Peter, or Kayla. In the last 18 months, these four Americans have been killed because our policy was strictly applied; whereas the five other Americans* (Casey Coombs, Sam Farren, Scott Darden, Theo Curtis, and Sgt. Bergdahl) who were negotiated for, by us or others, have returned home safely. This inconsistent implementation of our American hostage policy is unacceptable.

Additionally, we were deceived as an American family. We were told repeatedly that Jim was their highest priority. We trusted in our government to help him return home. During the brief month that Jim's ISIS captors reached out to negotiate for his release, our government refused to directly engage with the ISIS captors, leaving us alone as parents, to try to negotiate for our son's freedom!

Eighteen months after Jim's kidnapping, our family and the three other families of hostages held with Jim in Syria were threatened three times by Colonel Mark Mitchell, a member of our National Security Council, with prosecution by our government (though there was no precedent) if we attempted to raise a ransom to free our loved ones. He also told us very clearly that our country would not ask allies to help negotiate their release and would not conduct a military operation to rescue them. He made it very clear that USG planned to abandon these four Americans.

Thus in May of 2014, it became frighteningly clear that Jim, Peter, Steven and Kayla were considered "collateral damage" and that we families were totally on our own. I had spent much of our family savings and quit my job as a nurse practitioner to travel monthly to Washington to beg for help for Jim, to the United Nations and countless embassies asking for help and to Europe to speak to the freed hostages all to no avail. While our US Senators reached out and were sympathetic, we never even heard from our US Congressman. The Foley family did try to raise a ransom for Jim's release, in spite of threats of prosecution. But we started too late and were unable to raise enough money to interest ISIS. The reality is that few American families would be able to raise the ransom needed to actually free their loved ones.

Our US government refused to engage at a high level with our allies, who also had citizens held by ISIS. In the spring of 2014, a freed French hostage had specific information from ISIS to negotiate for our four American hostages and the three British ones; but our government refused to engage with the French or UK to save our citizens. The result is that all the European hostages are now home; whereas our son, the other Americans and British were brutally killed.

Though we had specific information regarding the exact locations of their captivity beginning in the fall of 2013, a military mission was not attempted until July of 2014, after all the Europeans were safely home. We are sincerely grateful to the brave soldiers making the attempt, but it was much too late.

In our family's situation, our hostage policy prohibited our government from interacting in any way with Jim's captors...even investigating who our son's captors were. Had our government been allowed to engage the captors, perhaps vital intelligence about ISIS might have been gleaned. Our government's abandonment of our son Jim allowed their deaths to be used as propaganda for ISIS recruitment, thus strengthening and emboldening ISIS. It surely helped in their recruitment of other violent people who want to destroy us.

At one point there were more than 20 Western hostages held together by ISIS, all of whom were citizens of our allies. All of our European allies valued their citizens enough to negotiate for their freedom. Had Jim been French, Spanish, German, Italian, or Danish he would be alive today.

We form coalitions for war...why did we not engage with our allies to free all of the western hostages? I believe much stronger coalitions with our allies are essential to deal with the shrewdness and hatred of these terrorist groups. I fear that our posture of no engagement with Jim's ISIS captors led to our underestimation of their intelligence and their deep-seated hatred for the US. What if we had been shrewd enough to engage with Jim's Syrian captors in the fall of 2013, to learn all we could about them, instead of ignoring them. Is it ever wise to ignore enemies of freedom and justice?

Jim believed in America. He believed that our government valued him as a journalist and as a citizen. He was hopeful until the end of his 20-month captivity. But he and our family were truly abandoned by our government. How would you feel if your son or daughter had been in Jim's predicament and treated similarly?

Is an individual American citizen no longer valuable? Why were Jim and the other Americans in Syria treated as collateral damage?

Does our United States of America truly want to protect and prioritize the return of its American citizens? If so, I ask you, esteemed members of Congress, to hold our new Hostage Recovery Fusion Cell accountable for the return of our citizens and to mandate a thorough re-evaluation of our current hostage policy to ensure that it also it truly saves the lives of Americans.

Thank you.

Diane M. Foley

* "Two Americans freed in Yemen, but fate of third is unknown" – *Washington Post*, September 20, 2015
   "American journalist held by rebels in Yemen is freed" – *Washington Post*, June 1, 2015

Mr. POE. Thank you, Ms. Foley, very much.
Dr. Danti.

**STATEMENT OF MICHAEL D. DANTI, PH.D., ACADEMIC DIREC-
TOR OF CULTURAL HERITAGE INITIATIVES, THE AMERICAN
SCHOOLS OF ORIENTAL RESEARCH**

Mr. DANTI. Thank you, Chairman Poe and Ranking Member
Keating, for this opportunity to discuss terrorist financing through
antiquities trafficking.

It is an honor to be here among such esteemed company but, of
course, with a heavy heart and with very serious concerns.

Since the outbreak of the Syrian civil war in 2011 and sudden
expansion of the so-called Islamic State, or ISIS, in 2014, we have
witnessed the worst cultural heritage crisis since World War II.

On a daily basis cultural sites are being destroyed for tactical,
strategic, economic and ideological reasons. Antiquities and other
cultural property are being pillaged to finance continued conflict
and global terrorism.

As an archeologist who has worked in Syria and Iraq for the last
25 years, there is not a day that goes by when I don't anguish over
the current plight of the Syrian and Iraqi people and the atrocities
ISIS and other groups are committing.

My colleagues and I at the American Schools of Oriental Research work closely with Syrian and Iraqi cultural heritage experts
and other concerned parties who are daily risking their lives to
save heritage from systematic campaigns of cultural cleansing.

These brave heritage professionals understand the importance of
ensuring a brighter future by preserving the past and cultural diversity.

The current conflict in Syria and Iraq is a war over ideas and
cultural identity that is rapidly spreading to neighboring countries.

The project I direct, the American Schools of Oriental Research
Cultural Heritage Initiatives, constantly monitors the cultural heritage crisis in Syria and northern Iraq, implements heritage
projects in Syria and produces reports and conducts outreach for
the U.S. Government and the general public.

We have seen that most of the major combatants commit cultural
property crimes. But by far, ISIS is our greatest concern. Over the
last 16 months, ISIS has developed a highly organized approach to
looting, trafficking and selling antiquities and other cultural property for funding.

ISIS also brazenly destroys heritage places to promote its radical
ideology and gain media exposure.

There is no doubt that terrorists derive significant revenue from
looted ancient antiquities and stolen cultural property. Satellite imagery, in-country sources and open-source information support this
conclusion.

Information in antiquities recovered by U.S. Special Operations
forces during the Abu Sayyaf raid in May of this year proves ISIS
uses the illicit antiquities trade as an important source of revenue.

To ISIS, antiquities are a natural resource to be mined from the
ground or pilfered from cultural repositories. This criminal activity
has increased as other revenue streams such as oil have been targeted through air strikes or other counter measures.

Antiquities trafficking is difficult to target and for ISIS and other extremists it has the benefit of rewarding collaboration with employment.

Antiquities trafficking doesn't make as many enemies among the local population as other crimes but instead it exploits poverty and hopelessness. Also, antiquities serve as instruments for money laundering.

We don't know the total dollar values of the illicit antiquities trade. There are too many unknowns. But ISIS and other transnational criminal organizations certainly find it crucial to their operations and the financial and cultural costs of the destruction are manifest now and will have a cascading effect for generations to come.

The current crisis requires increased and improved capacities in the United States for cultural security and cultural diplomacy. We need a more proactive and nimbler approach that couples existing governmental and nongovernmental capacities.

High level coordination would greatly enhance this work and would facilitate containing, degrading and ultimately destroying ISIS and other radical groups and transnational criminal organizations operating in the Middle East, North Africa and beyond.

Reducing global market space for conflict antiquities should be one of our highest priorities. Legislation is pending in the House and Senate that would help to achieve these goals.

Ultimately, the best solutions for the current cultural heritage crisis in Syria and northern Iraq also contribute to alleviating the humanitarian crisis, promoting conflict resolution, strengthening counter terrorism efforts and fostering peace building.

Thank you.

[The prepared statement of Mr. Danti follows:]

THE FINANCE OF GLOBAL TERRORISM THROUGH CULTURAL PROPERTY CRIME IN SYRIA AND NORTHERN IRAQ

Dr. Michael D. Danti
Academic Director,
American Schools of Oriental Research Cultural Heritage Initiatives

Written Statement Submitted for Testimony Before the House Committee on Foreign Affairs — Subcommittee on Terrorism, Nonproliferation, and Trade (TNT)

November 17, 2015— "Terrorist Financing: Kidnapping, Antiquities Trafficking, and Private Donations"

EXECUTIVE SUMMARY

•Since August 2014, the American Schools of Oriental Research Cultural Heritage Initiatives (ASOR CHI) has been investigating cultural property crimes in Syria and northern Iraq through a cooperative agreement with the U.S. Department of State (NEA-PSHSS-14-001). ASOR CHI utilizes high-resolution satellite imagery, information from in-country sources, and open source data to provide the U.S. Government and the public with continual and comprehensive situational assessment of heritage issues in the conflict zone.

•The current conflict in Syria and northern Iraq ranks as the largest cultural heritage crisis since World War II with combatants regularly committing cultural atrocities that deepen the conflict and exacerbate the humanitarian crisis. In the case of the so-called Islamic State (ISIS, ISIL) and other radical Islamist groups, these crimes tactically, strategically, and monetarily support campaigns of cultural cleansing and global terrorism.

•The looting of archaeological sites represents the most frequently reported cultural heritage incident in Syria, and analyses of satellite images show widespread, intensive looting since 2011. Thefts from cultural repositories in Syria and Iraq represent infrequent but high impact crimes.

•ASOR CHI analysis shows that all major belligerents operating in the conflict zone engage in cultural property crimes; however, all lines of evidence indicate ISIS ranks as the most egregious and brazen offender. ISIS has developed an organized and systematic approach for exploiting portable cultural property as an important revenue stream, especially ancient antiquities.

• The current crisis requires increased and improved capacities in the United States for cultural security and cultural diplomacy. The Unites States needs a more concerted approach to cultural property protection involving a diverse range of governmental and nongovernmental actors. High-level coordination would greatly enhance this work and would facilitate degrading and ultimately destroying ISIS and other radical Islamist groups and transnational criminal organizations operating in the Middle East, North Africa, and beyond.

TERRORISM AND CULTURAL PROPERTY CRIME: THE ISIS DUAL-EXPLOITIVE MODEL

The profound repercussions of the Arab Spring and, in particular, the outbreak of the Syrian Civil War and attendant instabilities in northern Iraq, have precipitated the gravest cultural heritage crisis since World War II. Multiple factors are contributing to the daily loss of our global patrimony in the "Cradle of Civilization." While alleviating the humanitarian crisis, conflict resolution, and peacebuilding must constitute the leading edge of international support, cultural property protection forms an integral and inextricable component of these efforts, as well as counterterrorism and global security strategies.

The futures of Syria and Iraq are suffering systematic attacks as the conflict's key belligerents deliberately pillage and destroy heritage sites and commit acts of cultural cleansing, deepening the crisis and the costs of reconstruction. While all major belligerents commit, or are complicit in cultural property crimes, research conducted since August 2014 by the American Schools of Oriental Research Cultural Heritage Initiatives (ASOR CHI) reveals that the so-called Islamic State (ISIL, ISIS) ranks as the most egregious offender.[1] ISIS practices a dual-exploitive approach to cultural assets that supports the organization's ideological objectives and helps to meet its financial needs. ISIL propaganda deftly promotes and legitimizes this model with its followers within the overarching goal of establishing a caliphate.

The dual-exploitive approach pairs 1) the deliberate destruction of cultural assets, usually heritage places, to achieve ideological and strategic objectives and to gain media exposure, with 2) the acquisition and sale of cultural property for terrorist finance.[2] This strategy is ultimately rooted in ISIS's al-Qaeda origins but ISIS has adapted the use of cultural property crime to blunt the financial impact of counter-terrorism measures and to meet the objectives of its particular Jihadi-Salafi ideology.[3] Unlike al-Qaeda, this ideology has emphasized the targeting of the "near enemy" — other non-allied Muslims,

---

[1] Danti, M. (2015). Ground-Based Observations of Cultural Heritage Incidents in Syria and Iraq. *Near Eastern Archaeology*, *78*(3), 132–141. http://doi.org/10.5615/neareastarch.78.3.0132. Casana, J. (2015). Satellite Imagery-Based Analysis of Archaeological Looting in Syria. *Near Eastern Archaeology*, *78*(3), 142–152. http://doi.org/10.5615/neareastarch.78.3.0142 . The *Weekly Report Series* of the American Schools of Oriental Research Cultural Heritage Initiatives is available at http://www.asor-syrianheritage.org/weekly-reports/

[2] On the foreign policy implications and connections between conflict looting for profit, attacks on cultural identity, and terrorism see Nemeth, E. (2015). *Cultural Security. Evaluating the Power of Culture in International Affairs*. Imperial College Press.

[3] For Jihadi-Salafism see Meijer, R. (2013). Introduction. In *Global Salafism. Islam's New Religious Movement*, edited by R. Meijer, 1–32. Oxford: Oxford University Press.

especially Shia and Sufi, and the region's ethnic and religious minorities — as an important step to establishing a caliphate. This opens the door to liquidating the cultural assets of large segments of Syria and Iraq's populations through theft or destruction. ISIS also views antiquities as a natural resource to be harvested for profit. While other ideological successors of al-Qaeda such as Jabhat al-Nusra espouse the dual-exploitive approach, we possess few details regarding their financing of terrorism through cultural property crimes because of their higher degree of operational secrecy and their lower emphasis on disseminating heritage-related propaganda. In light of this, this statement largely focuses on ISIS. Looking to the future, understanding the ISIS dual-exploitive approach to cultural assets, and developing increasingly effective means to counter it, should be prioritized given this model rooted in Jihadi-Salafi ideology will continue to prevail within Islamist extremism.

While factions within the Syrian Regime, Syrian Opposition, and Kurdish cantons commit cultural property crimes, these groups acknowledge a shared interest in preserving cultural heritage, and in each case affiliated heritage groups are attempting to protect cultural assets under perilous conditions. Conversely, ISIS, Jabhat al-Nusra, and other Islamist extremists are predatory transnational criminal organizations espousing ideologies that embody the antithesis of cultural property protection. These Islamist extremists are waging a regional war on cultural diversity, and they are rapidly expanding their global reach. The United States and other nations are combating ISIS's use of cultural property as a source of funding, but more should be done now. In particular, high-level coordination of the broad spectrum of governmental and nongovernmental entities charged with protecting international cultural heritage would strengthen our efforts. Simultaneously, we should increase our capacities in cultural security and cultural diplomacy to meet the new challenges of ISIS and other extremist groups waging wars on culture.

THE GLOBAL ART MARKET AND ARCHAEOLOGICAL LOOTING

In recent years, we have witnessed a dramatic growth in the value of the art market driven by the shift of art and antiques from collectibles to popular financial investments. The European Fine Art Foundation (TEFAF) estimates the value of the 2014 global art market at ⁻51 billion.[4] This market is highly opaque, fragmented, and relatively unregulated at all levels. In the case of antiquities, which are highly prized as investments and status items, demand exceeds the modest legal supply. Transnational criminal

---

[4] McAndrew, C. (2015). *TEFAF Maastricht Art Market Report 2015. European Fine Art Foundation.*

organizations and, increasingly, terrorist groups provide a steady stream of stolen and looted art that is laundered into the public marketplace or sold through private channels. Law enforcement agencies typically rank art crime as the third or fourth highest-grossing criminal enterprise. The internet increasingly serves as an important new tool for marketing illicit art and antiquities, extending the reach of dealers in illicit cultural property and reducing some of the risks involved in marketing contraband.

As ISIS increased its footprint in Syria and northern Iraq in 2014, it gained access to thousands of archaeological sites, cultural repositories, private collections, and caches of illicit cultural property held by other combatants and criminal organizations. ISIS openly promotes the theft of cultural property from its opponents, banned cultural institutions, and ethnic and religious minorities within its territories. While recent analyses of high-resolution satellite imagery show severe looting across all of Syria[5], including areas under Syrian Regime, Opposition, Kurdish, and ISIS control, industrial-scale looting typifies ISIS controlled areas. Data on illicit Syrian and Iraqi antiquities reaching the market reveal a large number of items for sale from looted archaeological sites in ISIS territory, and in-country sources working with ASOR CHI regularly provide information on the heavy involvement of ISIS in organizing and supporting the looting, trafficking, and sale of antiquities. The ISIS trade in illicit antiquities is best documented by antiquities, documents, and photos recently recovered by U.S. Special Operations Forces during the Abu Sayyaf raid on May 15, 2015 in Al-Amr (eastern Syria).[6] This information proves ISIS utilizes a highly organized approach to obtaining and marketing antiquities, akin to their exploitation of other natural resources, and places a high value on directing these activities.

ISIS REVENUE STREAMS

ISIS and other terrorist organizations operating in the conflict zones of Syria and northern Iraq rely on a diverse assortment of criminal revenue streams to fund their activities.[7] With its territorial holdings and state-building ambitions, ISIS is especially dependent on maintaining a steady source of funding. Cultural property crimes — including the looting of archaeological sites and thefts from cultural repositories and

---

[5] Casana, J. (2015).
[6] "ISIL Leader's Loot," U.S. Department of State, Bureau of Educational and Cultural Affairs website.
http://eca.state.gov/cultural-heritage-center/iraq-cultural-heritage-initiative/isil-leaders-loot (accessed Nov. 11, 2015).
[7] Humud, C. E., Pirog, R., & Rosen, L. (2015). Islamic State Financing and US Policy Approaches. *Washington, DC: Congressional Research Service.*

private collections — rank high among these sources of revenue[8], although there are currently no publicly-available, reliable estimates of the value of this trade. Moving beyond dollar values, antiquities looting provides extremists with certain benefits with little of the vulnerabilities and potential repercussions of other criminal endeavors. Extortion/protection rackets and asset thefts from private citizens remain key sources of revenue for ISIS, but such activities disorient and anger the local populations ISIS seeks to control and risk fomenting rebellions among core Sunni groups. Such uprisings partly linked to criminal revenue streams plagued ISIS's predecessor Al-Qaeda in Iraq[9], and ISIS seems especially concerned with preventing *Sahwa* (Awakening) movements in its core territories of Raqqa and Mosul. Oil and gas production are lucrative, but airstrikes have reduced capacity.[10] As other revenues diminish, ISIS and other groups appear to have compensated through increasing cultural property crime. Cultural property crime is difficult to target through military means, and cultural property crimes provide ISIS with a means for rewarding supporters (e.g., employment in the illicit antiquities industry). ISIS justifies the use of cultural property as an exploitable natural resource through its radical Jihadi-Salafi ideology, and in turn these crimes serve as grist for its propaganda mill; however, with regard to antiquities ISIS is caught in a hypocrisy that reveals its true nature. Publicly the organization depicts itself as striving to stamp out all symbols of supposed polytheism and idolatry (Arabic *shirk*) and heresy (Arabic *bidaa*) to purify Islam, and so deliberately destroys heritage places it deems objectionable. Nevertheless, ISIS rarely destroys portable material culture that would be classifiable as *shirk* and instead aggressively stockpiles portable cultural property to be sold on the market, revealing that at its core the group is simply a transnational criminal organization. This ideological contradiction has not seemed to adversely impact ISIS, and the group has developed a holistic approach to cultural property crime that promotes its radical ideology, provides powerful propaganda, and helps meet its financial bottom line. As ISIS spreads and other groups emulate this apex jihadist group, our global cultural patrimony is increasingly jeopardized.

The ISIS Antiquities Trade

[8] For example, see "Terrorist Financing and the Islamic State," testimony of Matthew Levitt, Director, Stein Program on Counterterrorism and Intelligence, Washington Institute for Near East Policy, to the House Committee on Financial Services, November 13, 2014.
[9] Lister, C. (2014). Profiling the Islamic State. *Brookings Doha Center Analysis Paper*, (13), pp. 8–9. Bahney, B., Shatz, H. J., Ganier, C., McPherson, R., & Sude, B. (2010). *An Economic Analysis of the Financial Records of al-Qa'ida in Iraq*. Rand Corporation.
[10] Humud, C. E., Pirog, R., & Rosen, L. (2015), pp. 1, 4–6.

In northern Iraq, the frequency of archaeological looting has thus far been low relative to the number of archaeological sites under ISIS control. The low level of conflict-related looting in northern Iraq relative to neighboring Syria parallels pre-conflict conditions: looting typified many regions of pre-conflict Syria but was much rarer in northern Iraq.

In northern Iraq, ISIS has robbed houses of worship, private collections, and large cultural repositories such as the Mosul Museum, Mosul University, and Mosul's libraries and archives. ISIS has also publicly destroyed cultural property housed in many of these institutions, circulating video footage and photos on the internet and publishing stories in its magazine *Dabiq*. Nevertheless, deliberate destructions of antiquities and other valuable, portable cultural property have been rare relative to the amounts sold. ISIS usually destroys items that are too large or famous for easy smuggling or that are low in potential sale value. In other cases, such destructions are punitive acts: ISIS occasionally confiscates cultural property from unauthorized smugglers and publicly destroys it, particularly when the seizures were witnessed by the public. Deliberate destructions may also represent attempts to divert attention from the organization's preoccupation with plunder. ISIS's greed conflicts with its highly vaunted campaign of purifying Islam (*tasfiya*) of supposed corruptions and heresies (*bidaa*) as well as its doctrine of iconoclasm intended to promote the oneness of God (*tawhid*) through the destruction of *shirk*.

In Syria, ISIS and other terrorist groups have ransacked large numbers of cultural repositories, including museums, off-site museum storage facilities, libraries, houses of worship, private collections, and the storehouses of archaeological expeditions. Looting of archaeological sites has expanded dramatically in all zones of control since the start of the conflict in 2011. In ISIS-occupied territory, looting is rampant and often industrial in its intensity, employing metal detectors, heavy machinery, and large work crews. Syrian sources indicate that on occasion ISIS members loot high value discoveries themselves. In most instances, however, ISIS is indirectly involved in the looting, trafficking, and sale of antiquities. Gangs of looters operated in Syria prior to the outbreak of hostilities in 2011, and there were well-established trafficking networks for antiquities. ISIS has simply taken control of these existing networks and introduced regulatory mechanisms to extract profits that it legitimizes through its ideology. As ISIS has become more secure in its operations in various theaters, the organization has exercised tighter control over antiquities operations, establishing offices for the licensing of looting and the collection of antiquities and related revenues.[11] The organization collects varying fees and percentages of profits from those trafficking and selling antiquities. ISIS thus may derive revenue at three points in the illicit trade — looting, smuggling, and sales. In Syria, licensed looters are allowed to smuggle their finds and to attempt to sell items with varying percentages paid to ISIS.[12] In the Raqqa area, if looters fail to find buyers after a certain deadline, ISIS mandates the auction of antiquities. The majority of antiquities documented by ASOR CHI on the illicit market were offered for sale from Syria or Turkey. ISIL's loss of the important Tell Abyad-Akçakale border crossing between Syria and Turkey may have disrupted ISIL-affiliated trafficking networks, and there are early signs that smugglers are increasingly moving material to Lebanon to reach global markets.

Preliminary data on trafficking indicates Turkey and Bulgaria play a major role in the illicit trade connected to ISIS, but additional data on trafficking routes is needed. ASOR CHI has documented large numbers of antiquities in the low-to-middle value ranges because looters and dealers utilize digital photographs to market this material. Low ranking participants in the illicit trade are often willing to sell these photos once antiquities have been trafficked up-market or sold. Investigative journalists and others have easily obtained large collections of photos of antiquities by posing as buyers. Traditionally illicit cultural property from conflict zones would be cached for years or even decade before being marketed, but criminals are using the internet, social media, digital photographs, and peer networks to mass market material almost immediately across the globe. In some digital photos, artifacts are shown *in situ* (i.e., in their original archaeological contexts) to provide evidence of their authenticity. ASOR CHI and other groups have documented a staggering number of coins, ancient glass, metal objects, sculptures, mummified human remains, manuscripts, cylinder and stamp seals, cuneiform inscriptions, and ethnographic items on the illicit market. In some cases, these objects were stolen from cultural repositories or site museums and have been published and/or still bear their original registration numbers. We have also documented a large number of fakes and replicas on the market.

Reconstructing the value of this illicit cultural property to individual terrorist organizations is complicated by several factors, key among them determining price and establishing criminal origin. The prices paid for illicit cultural property provided by dealers should be considered highly inflated given the

---

[11] "Syrian 'Monuments Men' Race to Protect Antiquities as Looting Bankrolls Terror," *Wall Street Journal*, February 10, 2015.
[12] See for example "ISIS Antiquities Sideline," *New York Times*, September 2, 2014. ASOR CHI has obtained copies of several such licenses.

dealers' obvious incentive to maximize profits on future sales by citing exaggerated historic sale prices. Information obtained through the Abu Sayyaf raid provides some insight into the value of the trade over a short period of time in one region under ISIS control, and we need more data like this to develop a clearer picture of the value of this trade. Establishing the criminal origin of antiquities presents another special difficulty. Even when they are willing to discuss their operations, dealers in illegal antiquities are reluctant to divulge the sources of illicit cultural property, and individual lots of illicit antiquities are often mixed together and represent the looting of several terrorist/criminal networks, inserted fakes and replicas, and more modern stolen cultural property. Ultimately we should not fixate on monetary matters: any source of revenue controlled by ISIS or other Islamist extremists must be stifled. In the end, we must also recognize that the cultural impacts of these atrocities ultimately outweigh the financial ramifications.

EFFECTIVE COUNTERMEASURES

ISIS and other Islamist extremist groups and transnational criminal organizations operating in the Middle East and North Africa have developed a highly organized and ideologically grounded approach to liquidating cultural assets for terrorist finance and for attacks on cultural identity and enacting campaigns of cultural cleansing. In the United States, we must combat this dual-exploitive assault on our security and global patrimony on many fronts with a nimbler approach. Foremost our efforts must be proactive rather than responsive: this necessitates high-level coordination of diverse efforts within the United States, enhancements and increases in capacities for cultural security and cultural diplomacy, and the identification and targeting of key vulnerabilities in the trade in illicit cultural property.

Dealers in illicit cultural property from Syria and Iraq utilize the internet and peer networks to market contraband to prospective buyers worldwide. This reduces many of the traditional risks of this criminal activity; however, a key vulnerability is the digital trail left behind. This digital trail should be systematically collected and stored in a single repository for access by all groups engaged in due diligence in the marketplace, cultural property protection, and counter-terrorism efforts. Such a database would also prove invaluable for efficiently repatriating cultural property in the post-conflict period.

Ultimately, the best solutions for the current cultural heritage crisis in Syria and northern Iraq also contribute to alleviating the humanitarian crisis, promoting conflict resolution, strengthening counterterrorism efforts, and fostering peacebuilding. There is no either-or choice between saving human lives and preserving cultural heritage — the two are inseparable. Syrians and Iraqis are risking their lives daily to save their cultural legacy. We must do all we can to help them in this struggle against depravity.

Mr. POE. Thank you very much, Dr. Danti. Thank you all for being here today. I recognize myself for some questions.

It seems to me, and I may not have all of their sources of revenue, but we have heard that terrorist groups will do anything for money. They will steal, like the robberies of the banks in Iraq.

They will, as Mr. Cassara talked about—I call it money laundering. I am a former judge. I call that money laundering what you were talking about—cooking the books on trade. They make money off of antiquities.

They make money off of hostages and they make money off of their wealthy donors who want to send money to these terrorist groups. And there are probably a whole lot more.

Let me try to address a couple of issues. Ms. Foley, you gave us some remarkable information and if I understand the current status of American hostage law or procedure, the United States has always had a policy not to pay ransom.

Now it has changed that the government won't pay money for ransom but if families or individuals do that law will not be enforced as to that payment.

Is that your understanding of the current status?

Ms. FOLEY. Families, you know, in criminal activity—a family has never been prosecuted for paying ransom to criminals who have a loved one. So there is——

Mr. POE. That is what I am asking. So as far as you know, no family has ever been required——

Ms. FOLEY. No. I know that, because we researched it, because we finally realized we were on our own and we had to try to raise a ransom.

But of course we wanted to protect anyone, you know, who would care to help us. So there is no precedent for that, sir.

Mr. POE. So that portion of the law, as the President said, is not being enforced as to prosecute families that pay for ransom?

Ms. FOLEY. Well, it really was never meant to prosecute families. It was meant to——

Mr. POE. It has never—okay.

Ms. FOLEY [continuing]. Prosecute any groups that might pretend to be a charity and instead give money to finance terrorism or something. It was never meant to be——

Mr. POE. Was your son kidnapped for ransom or was he kidnapped as a propaganda tool or both?

Ms. FOLEY. That is a good question. Only God would know what might be—might have might have been in their heads. He was a Westerner.

They don't check passports when they kidnap people, sir. You know, he was obviously a Westerner. He had been in and out of Syria.

He had been there over a year and more and more of the jihadists had come in in 2012. Jim had made very good relations with a lot of the family there and was trying to expose the atrocities of the Assad regime so felt, you know, protected.

A lot of the rebels really welcomed journalists early on so that their plight might get out to the world. But some people——

Mr. POE. He was used as a propaganda tool, too, though, wasn't he?

Ms. FOLEY. I think—I think initially they wanted to make money off of him.

Mr. POE. Okay.

Ms. FOLEY. Oh, yes. Oh, yes. The propaganda only came when our Government would not engage in any way. Nobody would negotiate for him. No one cared. So they thought well, hey, we can make a spectacle of this. We can really use—get a lot of PR out of killing these Americans.

Mr. POE. Dr. Weinberg, let me ask you some questions about the Gulf States. I am going to be real specific here, probably going to hurt somebody's feelings in the Gulf States.

We have a military base in Qatar that we use to fly aircraft in the Middle East when we are engaged in military activities in Afghanistan or Iraq. Is that right?

Mr. WEINBERG. That is correct.

Mr. POE. So Qatar helps us out with that. But we know that Qatar has donors there—wealthy donors who give money to terrorist groups. Is that correct?

Mr. WEINBERG. It has certainly been correct in the past.

Mr. POE. Do we know who those donors are? Do we know their name, rank and serial number, so to speak?

Mr. WEINBERG. The United States has sanctioned a number of Qatari nationals——

Mr. POE. What does that mean—don't do this anymore? I mean, what is a sanction against a national in Qatar who gives money to terrorist groups?

Mr. WEINBERG. That is exactly the problem, sir. They——

Mr. POE. Don't do anything, don't do it again, it is not nice.

Mr. WEINBERG. And the problem is that they—the local government often doesn't do anything about it. In fact, I have seen not a single indication of Qatar prosecuting anybody and convicting them under terror finance laws that have been on the books.

Mr. POE. Do we pay to have our military base in Qatar?

Mr. WEINBERG. No. The Qataris pay for it.

Mr. POE. Okay. So you think Qatar is playing both sides?

Mr. WEINBERG. I think Qatar is absolutely playing both sides in this regard and I think the United States——

Mr. POE. So they harbor people who give money to terrorist groups but they also have a military base where the United States can go and attack terrorist groups?

Mr. WEINBERG. Yes, and individuals the United States has sanctioned live just down the road from where this U.S. base is and if the United States chose to do so it would not be too difficult to launch air strikes if we were convinced or, you know, conducted some sort of operation.

Mr. POE. You mentioned that the United States has the authority to go after these people who are contributing to foreign terrorist organizations.

Mr. WEINBERG. If it chooses to use that capacity it is hard to envision——

Mr. POE. To your knowledge—this is my last question—to your knowledge of those different—I have two questions.

How many people are we talking about that are contributing money to terrorist groups?

Mr. WEINBERG. The people sanctioned in Qatar, it is—you can count them on a single hand.

Mr. POE. It is not very many?

Mr. WEINBERG. No.

Mr. POE. And, second, have we ever extradited, prosecuted or taken out somebody who is giving money to terrorist groups, to your knowledge?

Mr. WEINBERG. Have we ever prosecuted, extradited? Well, the United States sought to capture Khalid Sheikh Mohammed from Qatari territory in the 1990s.

He was a senior al-Qaeda operative responsible for attacks linked to the 1998——

Mr. POE. Did we ever get him?

Mr. WEINBERG. He—according to former U.S. officials cited in press reports, a senior Qatari, either royal family member or government official, tipped him off and he fled the country when we went to find him.

Mr. POE. So my question is—just answer the question. Have we ever captured, extradited, brought back one of these moneybag guys who are giving money to terrorist groups to the United States to prosecute them?

Mr. WEINBERG. Well, ultimately we caught KSM himself, who was a senior money man as well as operational man. But we did it in Pakistan.

Mr. POE. All right. Mr. Keating from Massachusetts.

Mr. KEATING. Thank you, Mr. Chairman.

I think one of the most important things any of us can do as Americans is get to the root issues of what is going on even though it is dangerous, even though they risk their lives doing it and get that message out to the U.S. and the world.

And Ms. Foley, your son did that and your testimony—I think he inherited a lot of his courage from his mother but—and thank you for being here.

I know that there are things we can do tangibly in terms of antiquities. I know there are things we can do in terms of trade-based money laundering. I know there are things that we can do to sanction some countries. But it is really troubling on the issue of kidnapping, ransom.

Could you tell me a little bit about the James W. Foley Legacy Foundation you are so involved with, Ms. Foley? One of the things they do is hostage support. Could you describe what kind of work you do there and what the foundation is doing?

Ms. FOLEY. In truth, we are just beginning. Jim was very, as I said, concerned about people without a voice. So one of the big issues, obviously, I have been concerned about are American hostages.

They end up in a truly gray zone, and gray meaning that nobody knew whose job it was to try to get them out and no one really wanted to touch the issue. It is a hot potato.

So one of the first things we have done this past year is we have raised funds for something called Hostage U.S., which will be similar to Hostage U.K. which will support American families in this predicament.

But the James W. Foley Foundation wants to go further. We want our Americans home. So whereas Hostage U.S.—we are going to continue to support them because families need support but I couldn't have cared how I was treated if Jim were home and I really feel as Americans we need to be shrewder.

We need to find a way to get them home, and I recognize that it is complex because of our—because we certainly don't want to fund terrorists. But is it wise to not even engage these people? Then we don't have a clue.

We don't know what is going on. We don't know what they want. We don't know who they are and, you know, I don't think so. I just think we have to be a lot shrewder. Otherwise, we are going to be out of luck.

So as far as the foundation, yes, we are working very closely with the fusion cell and Lisa Monaco, Jen Easterley, trying to find ways to hold them accountable for gee, a lot of U.S. assets have been given now.

Fifty individuals have this mission to bring Americans home. None are home yet since they have been started.

Granted, it is new but I am concerned because I think their hands are tied in a lot of ways. So that is one thing.

The other issue is conflict journalism. These days—it used to be in World War II journalists and aid workers were off limits. People—they had a certain neutrality. Not so anymore.

I mean, journalists and aid workers are targets and we have to be aware of that. So as a democracy ourselves, unless we come together for global safety for people who are giving us information, who dare to go where many don't dare to go, that is a huge concern of ours.

So we are really—we are working with an international coalition for safety and journalism and continue to be concerned about children without access to education, because Jim loved children.

He really felt education was the only way to—for societies to get out of poverty. So we are looking at that.

Mr. KEATING. One of the things I hope we can do is not have others experience everything that your family experienced and as you go forward with the foundation's work if you could keep us informed about some of the areas you think that we can get involved with as you go forward.

Please do that. Feel free to do that because I think we can certainly do better.

Ms. FOLEY. We better do better, sir. You know, it is frightening if we can't do better in that regard.

Mr. KEATING. I agree, and thank you——

Ms. FOLEY. Thank you.

Mr. KEATING [continuing]. For that. Just another question for Dr. Danti. The May 15th raid on ISIL leader Abu Sayyaf—you called that a game changer at a certain point.

What did we learn from that that we didn't know before?

Mr. DANTI. We learned that antiquities were very important to the organization and they were the functional equivalent of other natural resources.

75

There were emails. There were documents indicating that Abu Sayyaf had been put in charge of that trade because it was important to the organization.

He was found to be in possession of hundreds of antiquities, some of them looted from the Mosul museum, and he also had, disturbingly, photographs of other high-end items on his laptop. Some of those items we had been tracking are known to have been sold through Turkey.

Mr. KEATING. Okay. I don't know if anyone else wants to comment on that briefly. But I will say this, that many times in this very turbulent time of terrorism we are so frustrated we put up our hands and we can say what can we do.

I think you four as witnesses have given us things we can do to further fight this effort and I appreciate it and I think these are very tangible real suggestions that can go forward on all fronts.

Thank you. I yield back.

Mr. POE. I want the members to know that we are in the midst of voting. We will continue after votes. We have one vote. But we will not recess until we have at least one more member ask questions and then we will come back. I apologize to our panelists but that one vote shouldn't take a long time.

Mr. Wilson from South Carolina.

Mr. WILSON. Ms. Foley, again, thank you for your courage, and as a former reporter myself so many points you have made—that indeed in other conflicts the journalists have been noncombatants.

But it is such a chilling reminder that we are dealing with illegal enemy combatants not in uniform. This is just so—to me, so extraordinarily unprecedented and putting the American people at risk, and we are at a time even today, within the last 48 hours, that ISIL Daesh issued a statement that Washington and Rome are the next targets and so we have just got to be vigilant.

That is why I appreciate the point that you are making too that where we all support no concession, no tribute, that doesn't mean not negotiate. So I—you are making a difference by raising these issues.

And then it is appalling to me that there was not an effort of military rescue. Was there any reason—particularly when you indicate that it was an exact location of 20 together.

With that information, it is just appalling to me that action was not taken. And that is one question. Then the next question why was that not done, and then, you know, with the attack in Benghazi we are still discussing who did it. What? This should be determined, and then there should be efforts to find them.

So on both—why was there no action and what is the status of determining who these murderers are.

Ms. FOLEY. Well, those are all good questions—questions that I truly don't have the answers for.

All I know is an American citizen—we started to have eye-witnesses as of fall—early fall of 2013 of exactly where Jim was and our Government knew that there were three other Americans and British with him and where—quite sure that they also realized how many other of allies were also together because slowly the other—their allies were negotiating all of these people out.

Jim had already been held a whole year before all these other peoples were added. Jim was one of the first—Jim and British citizen John Cantlie and, of course, Austin Tice, who was taken in August 2012.

They were the first ones that I know of that were taken in Syria. But then gradually all these others were taken, most of them in later in 2013, and—but the other European countries got right on it and started negotiating with the captors so that their citizens came out.

As far as where they were held, we had information throughout starting in the fall of 2013 and then again December 2013. They were moved, but because hostages started coming out in early 2014 we were—we received very detailed information.

As a matter of fact, it became clearer and clearer as the spring of 2014 went on because these European hostages came out with very specific information and some of them—one Italian citizen came to the U.S. twice on his own dime trying to get somebody to hear the specifics he had in terms of exact location of where they were being held.

But no one wanted to hear it, and this—particularly Federico came more than any of the others. Some of the others hesitated to do that because their governments had figured out a way to get them out.

So they, understandably, expected our Government to work with theirs to collaborate, if you will, to get our citizens out. But it didn't happen, sir.

Mr. WILSON. Well, and it is inconceivable with the released captives that there couldn't be an effort to determine who the perpetrators are and so——

Ms. FOLEY. Don't you think? I agree with you. I am appalled as an American, sir.

Mr. WILSON. Well, I want to work with our chairman and get this straight. So thank you very much. I yield.

Mr. POE. The Chair will now go to Mr. Higgins for his statement.

Mr. HIGGINS. Thank you, Chairman.

Mr. POE. Or questions. Excuse me.

Mr. HIGGINS. Ms. Foley, in your testimony you had indicated that you and your family were left to negotiate with your son's captors. With whom would you negotiate and what was the nature of that discussion?

Ms. FOLEY. Well, the only—the only opportunity we had, Mr. Higgins, was for a month in 2013 end of November we out of the blue got an email saying that they had Jim and they would send us—they wanted some questions, proof of life. Pardon?

Mr. HIGGINS. Who is—who is they?

Ms. FOLEY. They really didn't want us to know. They said they were Syrian rebels. They didn't identify themselves anymore than that.

Mr. HIGGINS. So they initiated contact with you and your family?

Ms. FOLEY. Mm-hmm. Absolutely. But it was through a very encrypted email that our FBI had no way of tracking. So they are very shrewd, sir. Very shrewd. They knew how to reach us but we didn't know how to reach them.

Mr. HIGGINS. So you couldn't respond back?

Ms. FOLEY. Well, I could—I could only respond through that email. But what I meant to say is we couldn't find out who was sending it. It was obvious that they were English speaking, however, because, you know, of the command of language.

Mr. HIGGINS. And was there specifics about a ransom number or conditions?

Ms. FOLEY. When they initially reached out to us, yes, it was ridiculous—like, it was—they wanted 100 million euro or all Muslim prisoners kind of thing and, you know, FBI—you know, of course, we right away sent it to FBI and they just said, oh, keep them talking—keep them talking.

But within a few emails when they realized they were just talking to the family they had absolutely no interest and so they cut off discussions until the only other time, sir, was when the French came out in March 2014 they came out with another very specific offer to negotiate for all Americans and all the British.

Mr. HIGGINS. And your primary source of contact in the United States was the FBI?

Ms. FOLEY. We had no primary source. I did have one—we had one FBI agent who debriefed me all the time. But——

Mr. HIGGINS. Debriefed you on what?

Ms. FOLEY. Anything. I mean, I was—I was talking to anybody—all the freed hostages that I could. I said earlier a lot of times FBI couldn't even get to them. So——

Mr. HIGGINS. At any point during your ordeal did you get a sense that your son was going to be freed at some point or——

Ms. FOLEY. Not at all. However, our Government told me, anyone I talked to at State or FBI, that Jim was the highest priority. So we were deceived throughout the first 18 months.

Mr. HIGGINS. You never believed that?

Ms. FOLEY. Oh, I believed it totally, sir.

Mr. HIGGINS. How long——

Ms. FOLEY. That is why I didn't—we didn't try to raise ransom or do anything privately. Oh, we totally believed it.

Mr. HIGGINS. When did you stop believing it?

Ms. FOLEY. By the—by the late spring of 2014 when I could—primarily when Mark Mitchell threatened us three times and made it very obvious that our Government was going to do nothing for those citizens.

Mr. HIGGINS. And what was the nature of Mark—what was his—what was his threat?

Ms. FOLEY. Oh, that first of all as Americans if we dared to raise a ransom to get our loved ones out we would definitely be prosecuted and, secondly, there is no way our Government would ever ask another country.

You know, he was going by the law and I know that the law says we are not—you know, we don't want Qatar to do these things and I—but what he was saying essentially is your government will do nothing to get your people out. Nothing.

And he just said it in a very—I mean, God bless that man anyway. I don't know. It is just very appalling that as an American that we would do nothing for some of the best of America, some of our journalists, some of—people who care about the suffering of the people in Syria.

It was appalling to me, sir.

Mr. HIGGINS. I have no further questions.

Mr. POE. I thank the gentleman from New York.

We will be in a short recess until the members vote and quickly come back and we will continue this.

I want to thank the witnesses for your patience. But your information is so important that we don't want to—I don't want to end this hearing at this point.

So we will be in recess until—for 15 minutes maximum.

[Recess.]

Mr. POE. The subcommittee will reconvene.

The Chair recognizes the gentleman from California, Mr. Sherman.

Mr. SHERMAN. Thank you.

Qatar doesn't just allow its citizens to give money to terrorist groups. Government money is going to Hamas and other terrorist groups.

I think we have to get serious about this war. I will give you some examples of where at least some of our friends are not serious.

The Iraqi Government pays salaries to former civil servants who live in ISIS-controlled areas. I do not remember General DeGaulle sending gold coins to French teachers in Normandy or Bordeaux.

The oil fields controlled by ISIS we don't bomb. We bombed World War II oil fields. We don't bomb these. Some say it is because the Iraqis want to get them back intact. Some say it is because the Iraqi Government is making a lot of money on this war and doesn't want to see ISIS lose the revenue.

But you have something which by the definitions of a war we took most seriously—World War II—is a strategic target. We know that ISIS is pumping the oil. We hit their mobile refineries but we won't hit the oil fields.

We are not hitting the dams. We are not hitting their electric generation facilities and I can't get a straight answer out of either our Government or the Iraqi Government as to whether Iraq is providing free electricity to Mosul.

But the lights are on for—and they are not on all the time but they are on for a reason. The biggest score—and I realize it may be slightly outside the definition of this hearing, although we do have the word donations in this—is ISIS has got its hands on $500, $800 million of Iraqi currency.

Now, what other countries do for various reasons is that they issue new currency. You do a recall of the greenbacks and you issue bluebacks.

Iraq didn't do that because that is a technique that is used to go after corrupt politicians and organized crime and when you have a Baghdad government installed by us, protected by us, financed with our money that is pretty dependent upon, infiltrated by, controlled by Iran, the Quds Forces and organized criminal and corrupt elements, they are not going to recall the currency.

So the—as to hostages, we definitely should not do nothing. The raid didn't work but it shows a U.S. determination. We need to sanction Iran for holding five American hostages.

The President made it clear that the deal in Geneva related only to nuclear weapons and if any other country was holding five of our hostages we would—we would certainly sanction them.

Dr. Weinberg, does Qatar even pretend to outlaw voluntary contributions made by its citizens to Hamas? Is that a violation of Qatari law?

Mr. WEINBERG. So Qatari law doesn't discuss specific organizations in terms of the legislation. They have had several laws on the books, one actually approved by the emir this week banning individual—banning citizens from collecting money without authorization for donations.

But this is the——

Mr. SHERMAN. Well, that is collecting from others. What—is it illegal to just send your money directly—Hamas donation fund care of Gaza?

Mr. WEINBERG. The Qatari Government has given itself the authority to list terrorist groups or——

Mr. SHERMAN. Have they listed any?

Mr. WEINBERG. Not to my knowledge. There—of the four laws intended to combat terrorism finance in the country the U.S. has yet to see serious convictions under——

Mr. SHERMAN. So it is illegal to give money to anyone on the list, and the list is a blank piece of paper?

Mr. WEINBERG. The latest law, theoretically, means that you need to get governmental authority to collect donations for anybody. The question is——

Mr. SHERMAN. To collect. But if—I mean, it is—if Qataris see that there is a disaster in Bangladesh and they give to the Bangladeshi Red Crescent Society or the—or UNICEF or something like that, they don't need government permission to write a check to UNICEF, do they?

Mr. WEINBERG. The—I think the most striking evidence in this regard is that the United States sanction to Qatari nationals in August, I believe, who, as I understand it, were running the most high profile fund-raising organization for Syria relief in Qatar.

The U.S. alleged that they both were high level al-Qaeda financial operatives. It took the Qataris almost a year after the organization was allegedly, according to the Washington Post, endorsed by the Nusra Fund on social media for the Qataris to shut it down and a year after that when the U.S. actually sanctioned them, U.S. officials indicated the Qataris still had not arrested the two men.

Mr. SHERMAN. Nor would we expect them to. I would point out to our friends in Qatar that just because you host a U.S. military base does not mean that the United States has to preserve your regime.

We have a military base in Cuba. That doesn't mean we are supporters of the government in Havana—our policies changed from this way or that way. But it is nice to have the base there. That doesn't mean we have to support their government.

I would also point out, and with Ms. Foley here, you know, I feel bad saying it but I don't think that we should be allowing—paying money—give ransom to terrorist organizations.

From an emotional standpoint you want to. From an emotional standpoint it may get your—the particular loved one back. But it

is just a while before they kill some other Americans or seize some other American hostages and, of course, with money that gives them both an incentive and a capacity.

So I yield back and thank you for time.

Mr. POE. The Chair recognizes Mr. Keating from Massachusetts.

Mr. KEATING. Thank you, Mr. Chairman.

A question about the nonprofit again—not just Qatar but particularly, Mr. Cassara, Dr. Weinberg, what other nonprofits are there in the world?

Are some people donating unwittingly, not knowing where some of the money is going? Are we able to do this? If you could, just enlighten us on some of those sources of financing——

Mr. WEINBERG. Sure. Absolutely.

Mr. KEATING [continuing]. That the terrorists get.

Mr. WEINBERG. So this has been a longstanding practice among financiers of—financial operatives for al-Qaeda for years, which is basically while we can't openly practice what we do in many regards so let us cloak it in a veneer of charitable relief.

There is a particularly noteworthy case in Kuwait as well and there was a fund-raising outfit operated by an individual named Hajjaj al-Ajmi, which was presenting itself in most of its presentations as relief for the Syrian people, support for legitimate resistance.

But in practice, according to what the U.S. Government has designated, he was basically funding al-Qaeda in very large amounts and since then he has been called in for questioning by Kuwaiti authorities——

Mr. KEATING. Are donors aware—are some of them innocently being——

Mr. WEINBERG. Some of them are innocently being exploited. There are—the—this tribe in Kuwait as well as another tribe have been exploited by people trying to play on their sympathies.

The challenge is that once these sorts of frauds are exposed the penalties are inconsistent at best in some of these places.

And so the United States can work to try and build leverage to motivate the host governments to act because apparently so far they don't seem to be sufficiently consistently motivated.

Mr. KEATING. And I imagine if you just go with a nonprofit name and not the people behind, sort of like Whac-A-Mole because they can do this and start another nonprofit.

Mr. WEINBERG. Exactly. One of—in that instance one of the individuals—that individual is under sanctions but his co-captain in one of his main fund-raising networks is still a senior operative in a Kuwaiti political party.

Mr. KEATING. Dr. Danti, just quickly. I am curious, too. With the—you know, the passageway for the antiquities what are some of the transit countries involved?

What is being done there and are they following the say routes of other illicit activities like drugs or money laundering?

Are there parallels and how can we—I think we can do things here at home to, you know, tamp down on demand, talk to people in the U.K. similarly, you know, motivated to do that in terms of final destinations but what about the transit companies—countries, rather, and what about—what can we do to disrupt that chain?

81

Mr. DANTI. Right. So in the cases that we have seen over the last 16 months, the primary trafficking points were antiquities coming out of Syria were Lebanon and Turkey, and from that point much of the material was going to Bulgaria and Greece and then with the objective of moving the material into the Schengen zone—the free border zone.

Those are the cases that we were looking at. There were allegedly routes taking material to Jordan, Israel and the Gulf as well.

Since, let us say, October some of those routes have shifted as the Turks have taken military action. Some of the border crossings that Islamic State was using have fallen to YPG, or Turkish forces, and we see initial indicators that some of the Sunni Arab and Islamic State ISIS trafficking is moving out toward Lebanon.

There has been a shift in the markets there presumably to take the material from Lebanon to either Cyprus, Greece or Bulgaria.

I would say that in terms of trying to shut that trade down what could be done is to limit the number of ports that are involved in illicit trade in antiquities and also to limit the number of people who can legally import antiquities.

Mr. KEATING. Are they following other illicit activities like drugs or money laundering? Any of those?

Mr. DANTI. Yes. In looking at the—into the routes that the material was taken through Turkey and Bulgaria it was following a lot of other contraband out of the country—for example, stolen automobiles, their stolen capital goods, and following the routes that fighters—Islamic State fighters were entering the country through and in illegal weapons the same border crossings—for example, the Tell Abyad-Akçakale border crossing that the—that ISIS told its would-be migrants to use to come and join the caliphate in a PDF that was posted online.

Satellite imagery, in-country sources indicated that was a route that the antiquities were leaving the country from to ports in western Turkey and in southern and western Turkey where Islamic State essentially is surely alighting with or joining up with organized crime units within Turkey to move that.

Islamic State is essentially new management taking advantage of existing looting networks and existing trafficking networks that predate the conflict period and they have essentially just encouraged additional—far more looting and trafficking of antiquities.

But these routes existed in the pre-conflict period.

Mr. KEATING. Just quickly, any human trafficking involved in that?

Mr. DANTI. Not that I am aware of.

Mr. KEATING. Okay. Thank you. I yield back, Mr. Chairman.

Mr. POE. Chair recognizes the gentleman from New York.

Mr. HIGGINS. Thank you, Mr. Chairman.

I just—you know, kidnapping for ransom has, you know, become a significant source of terror financing. In 2003, al-Qaeda would get about $200,000 per hostage. Now, they are getting about $10 million.

Over half of al-Qaeda's operating revenue comes from ransom from kidnapping. But ISIS seems to be different. ISIS seems to be involved in other activity and a lot of their ability to raise funds is locally—terrorizing the local population, taxing people.

Every activity that is done there is taxed and results in a revenue source for ISIS. Any thoughts about that distinction and what is gleaned from it? Anybody on the panel.

Mr. WEINBERG. So I think it is—it is certainly important to contextualize this, like you said, and to say that the primary sources of revenue that ISIS in particular have are derived from controlled local territory.

I think it is also important for us to recognize that Treasury has indicated ISIS as well as branches of al-Qaeda in Yemen and north Africa have been able to conquer territory in part because they have used private donations as well as ransoms to fuel and to fund that territorial conquest.

Particularly as the United States and our allies work to cut off their income from oil smuggling and from other—and from their ability to even hold territory in the first place they are going to fall back on these other sorts of revenue as well. And so if we really want to conquer this phenomenon we need to address this.

We have also learned that ISIS and al-Qaeda frequently will use these private donations and other sorts of external funding to particularly pay for moving recruits from other countries, which they have done in the tens of thousands, to battle zones. And so if we can cut off these two other sources of funding we may be able to limit the abilities—the ability of the organization to function even if it still has other sources of revenue.

Mr. CASSARA. It is not only sources of funding, it is laundering money. I would just like to share a quick anecdote.

About 2002, not too long after 9/11, I had a conversation with a Pakistani gentleman who I guess you could charitably describe works in the gray markets.

And I was talking to him about things we are talking about today. I was talking to him about trade-based money laundering, over and under valuation, hawala, the misuse of the Afghan transit trade, et cetera, et cetera.

And he finally turns to me, he says, Mr. John, he says, don't you know that your enemies are transferring money in value right under your noses but the West doesn't see it. Your enemies are laughing at you.

And I think that kind of encapsulated a lot of what this issue is all about. We have spent an incredible amount of time the last 14 years since 9/11 looking in many of the wrong places.

We have been concentrating on financial intelligence, setting up financial intelligence units, filing suspicious activity reports, sanctions and designations. We are a nation of laws.

Our adversaries, the terrorists, they are not. They are laughing at us, okay. We need to start thinking how they operate, all right. We need to understand their cultures, their methods of doing business, their values.

We are making progress but it has taken far too long. I think we are kind of emphasizing the wrong things. Just an observation.

Ms. FOLEY. I would concur with that in a big way. I mean, I just feel that they have the upper hand because they are shrewder.

They are—they have studied us. They know how to use Twitter. They know how to use PR, video, et cetera, to get their message, to recruit people who hate us, and we—you know, we won't even talk to them.

I mean, we have got to know our enemies. We have got to use our cultural expertise to really get serious about engaging with us.

You know, I mean that is why, you know, I realize Jim was just a young American but he—they didn't—our FBI and State didn't use that situation with four Americans being held there to find out who are these people that are holding our four Americans.

Why are they holding our—what do they want? They didn't even try, and how are we going to understand and engage this enemy if we don't even try to know them? Thank you.

Mr. HIGGINS. Yield back.

Mr. POE. Chair recognizes himself for two more questions in closing.

In addition to the list we started out making about where terrorist organizations get their money we have to now add wildlife poaching is another way they get their money, and as my friend from New York mentioned, human trafficking—they make money off of human trafficking as well and charities.

Let me ask you something, Dr. Weinberg. You mentioned specifically about charities in other countries. Do we have charities in the United States that are not really charities—they are just a front for money laundering or donations that go to charity but ends up in the hands of these bad guys?

Mr. WEINBERG. Yes. The—most recently U.S. law enforcement authorities I believe pressed charges against a network of several Yemeni nationals who were using illicit methods within the United States to fund-raise for al-Qaeda in the Arabian Peninsula including defrauding credit card companies, taking out money and then closing down the accounts.

Also, if you look back historically Hamas used U.S. territory quite deftly in methods that were exposed during the Holy Land Foundation trial and many of those individuals have gone on abroad—people who are linked to the Holy Land Foundation—to continue to be parts of Hamas' regional financial network including one case I identified in my written testimony.

Mr. POE. And once again, the handful of individuals who do most of the contributing to foreign terrorist organizations, giving them money, we know who those people are.

Is that right or not?

Mr. WEINBERG. Sometimes.

Mr. POE. We know who some of them are?

Mr. WEINBERG. Right. Part of— part of the challenge is that the donors are often harder to track down than the operators themselves, right.

If you look at it almost as a pyramid or something——

Mr. POE. I understand.

Mr. WEINBERG. Right. But if you take out the people in the middle——

Mr. POE. Like in a drug trafficking we get the guy who is selling drugs on the corner. We don't get the guy who is bringing it into the country or making the money.

Mr. WEINBERG. Exactly. The more we can take out the operatives in the middle. The people at the bottom of the period are more prone to sting operations and things like that.

Mr. POE. And Mr. Cassara, going back to your comments, United States has a financial investigation of money going from banks to banks, trying to track it to see if it is legitimate or not.

But your testimony—the terrorists don't operate that way. Is that—is that a fair statement? They operate through trade and how much illicit money have they been making with the money laundering through trade that you discussed?

Mr. CASSARA. First of all, I would like to explain that, as we have talked about here today, terrorists are adversaries. They diversify just like any criminal organization does, just like—just like a good investor does, if you will.

You don't put all your eggs in one basket. They diversify. So they use a wide variety of funding methods and laundering methods.

Yes, they use banks. They do. But I think there has been an overemphasis on us targeting Western-style financial institutions.

In effect, we are still fighting the war on drugs where large amounts of dirty money sloshed around through Western financial institutions. In fact, our anti-money laundering counter measures were put in place, you know, a generation ago when we were fighting the war on drugs. We have to be a little bit more nimble right now. Yes, I believe trade is a huge issue. The Financial Action Task Force calls it one of the three largest money laundering methodologies in the world.

Mr. POE. How much money are we talking about?

Mr. CASSARA. You are talking—the magnitude of money laundering in general, according to the International Monetary Fund, is about 3 to 5 percent of the world GDP or, roughly speaking in rough numbers, say, $5 trillion a year, okay—roughly, the size of the U.S. budget.

Mr. POE. Give or take a trillion or two?

Mr. CASSARA. Give or take a trillion or two. You are talking real money here. They further think that is about equally divided between—talking suspicious—SUAs, suspicious unlawful activities, predicate offenses to charge money laundering, the criminal side—fraud, antiquities smuggling, human trafficking, narcotics, et cetera, and tax evasion.

So it is about equally divided. Say, it is $4 trillion a year—about $2 trillion tax evasion and about $2 trillion traditional criminal predicate offenses. How much of that involves trade-based money laundering, my personal opinion is, and I detail that in this book, is—that is the largest money laundering methodology in the world.

But we don't know because it has never been systematically examined. We haven't done it in the United States. Our Department of Treasury has never taken a look at it.

I mean, the Financial Action Task Force did a money laundering methodology back about 2006 and, you know, they kind of threw up their hands.

But this—it is not a solvable problem but it is something that we can do a great deal more to combat because the data exists in many hidden money laundering systems methodologies out there

today. Say, for example, bulk cash smuggling—it is very, very difficult to follow that trail.

But this type of thing has data and with modern analytics today we can do a much better job.

Mr. POE. All right. I want to thank all four of you for being here. Oh, you want to ask some more questions?

Mr. SHERMAN. Yes.

Mr. POE. Mr. Sherman.

Mr. SHERMAN. I am inspired by this work. I just want to bring to the attention of the subcommittee it is not just Qatar that takes a blind eye. It is also the U.S. Government.

I brought to the attention of both the attorney general and the IRS the fact that there is a group based in Britain called Viva Palestinia that gives money to Hamas.

Now, you got to understand that in liberal circles it is kind of—very liberal leftist circles—it is kind of acceptable to give money to Hamas.

It is not al-Qaeda, not ISIS but Hamas, okay. And so brought to their attention the Viva—and then the Web site of the Interreligious Foundations for Community Organization that said we will help you get a tax deduction for giving money to Viva Palestinia so that they can give the money to Hamas.

Brought this to their attention. Not only was there no criminal action taken but after 5 years there is just a review of the Interreligious Foundations and if there is anybody in this room who wants to give a—get a tax deduction and give money that they can be certain will go to Hamas the Web site is available to you right now.

So I know we are the international affairs committee and we criticize a lot of foreign governments. Our own is in this, and I will say this.

The IRS has published the fact that they are doing a study on this and they may eventually turn to the Interreligious Foundation for Community Organization.

In spite of the fact that it has the word interreligious in it and deny their 501(c)(3) status, maybe by then we will see peace in the Middle East and Hamas won't be a problem.

Second, on cultural awareness I know Ms. Foley brought that up. I have been on—the double entendre would be I have been on a jihad to get the State Department to hire just a few people who are hired not because they can pass the Foreign Service exam but because they are real experts in the theology and jurisprudence of Islam because you do have to understand not just your enemy but the group that we are trying to win over, which is the 1.2, 1.3 billion Muslims who ISIS would like to win over to their side.

And they are pretty rigid over there. You know, if you go to Princeton they will hire you but if your knowledge—if you reach one of the highest levels of knowledge in the theology and jurisprudence of Islam they won't and so their arguments are basically to tell people ISIS is bad because they kill men, women and children Yazidis without being in a position to argue as to whether—to deal with the argument from ISIS that—well, that is a good thing. Look at their twisted interpretation of Islamic jurisprudence and theology.

So just when we—while we criticize other governments we have got a government that will still to this day give you a tax deduction for giving money that you know goes to Hamas and we do have some people in the State Department that know some things about Islam, whatever you can learn kind of from the outside in a couple of graduate seminars, and we have religious Muslims but they may be working on trade issues.

There is no department there that says here is how we can frame our arguments to Islamic governments based on—based on a real knowledge of Islam.

With that, I think I have gone over time. I yield back. I haven't gone—I am yielding back a minute early. Put that on the record. Thank you.

Mr. POE. I will put it down because that is a record.

But I do want to thank the Members of Congress. I want to thank you all for being here. I can't emphasize enough how valuable the information that you have given us is.

We—Ranking Member Keating and I were talking during the break that we could have a hearing on each one of the issues that the four of you talked about because it is important information and we appreciate the fact that you have been here and have given us this information.

Once again, Ms. Foley, thank you so much for being here. I agree with the comment that was made—your son probably got his spunk from you, which is—that is a compliment, by the way.

So I thank all of you all and if you have any other information that you would like to share with the committee feel free to do that. Give it to me and I will share it with the other members of the committee.

The committee now is adjourned.

[Whereupon, at 4:10 p.m., the subcommittee was adjourned.]

A P P E N D I X

MATERIAL SUBMITTED FOR THE RECORD

SUBCOMMITTEE HEARING NOTICE
COMMITTEE ON FOREIGN AFFAIRS
U.S. HOUSE OF REPRESENTATIVES
WASHINGTON, DC 20515-6128

Subcommittee on Terrorism, Nonproliferation, and Trade
Ted Poe (R-TX), Chairman

TO: MEMBERS OF THE COMMITTEE ON FOREIGN AFFAIRS

You are respectfully requested to attend an OPEN hearing of the Committee on Foreign Affairs, to be held by the Subcommittee on Terrorism, Nonproliferation, and Trade in Room 2200 of the Rayburn House Office Building (and available live on the Committee website at http://www.ForeignAffairs.house.gov):

DATE: Tuesday, November 17, 2015

TIME: 2:00 p.m.

SUBJECT: Terrorist Financing: Kidnapping, Antiquities Trafficking, and Private Donations

WITNESSES: Mr. John Cassara
                   (Former Special Agent, U.S. Department of the Treasury)

                   David Andrew Weinberg, Ph.D.
                   Senior Fellow
                   Foundation for Defense of Democracies

                   Mrs. Diane Foley
                   Founder
                   James W. Foley Legacy Foundation Inc.

                   Michael D. Danti, Ph.D.
                   Academic Director of Cultural Heritage Initiatives
                   The American Schools of Oriental Research

By Direction of the Chairman

The Committee on Foreign Affairs seeks to make its facilities accessible to persons with disabilities. If you are in need of special accommodations, please call 202/225-5021 at least four business days in advance of the event, whenever practicable. Questions with regard to special accommodations in general (including availability of Committee materials in alternative formats and assistive listening devices) may be directed to the Committee.

COMMITTEE ON FOREIGN AFFAIRS

MINUTES OF SUBCOMMITTEE ON _____ *Terrorism, Nonproliferation, and Trade* _____ HEARING

Day_____ *Tuesday* _____ Date_____ *November 17* _____ Room_____ *2200* _____

Starting Time_____ *2:21 p.m.* _____ Ending Time_____ *4:10 p.m.* _____

Recesses | *1* | (*3:24* to *3:40*) (___ to ___) (___ to ___) (___ to ___) (___ to ___) (___ to ___)

Presiding Member(s)

Chairman Ted Poe

Check all of the following that apply:

Open Session [✓]
Executive (closed) Session [ ]
Televised [✓]

Electronically Recorded (taped) [✓]
Stenographic Record [✓]

TITLE OF HEARING:

Terrorist Financing: Kidnapping, Antiquities Trafficking, and Private Donations

SUBCOMMITTEE MEMBERS PRESENT:

Reps. Poe, Keating, Wilson, Sherman, Cook, Higgins, Perry, Castro, Ribble, Kelly

NON-SUBCOMMITTEE MEMBERS PRESENT: *(Mark with an * if they are not members of full committee.)*

HEARING WITNESSES: Same as meeting notice attached? Yes [✓] No [ ]
(If "no", please list below and include title, agency, department, or organization.)

STATEMENTS FOR THE RECORD: *(List any statements submitted for the record.)*

SFRs - Chairman Poe on behalf of Dr. David Weinberg and Colonel Mark E. Mitchell

TIME SCHEDULED TO RECONVENE _____
or
TIME ADJOURNED _____ *4:10 p.m.* _____

Subcommittee Staff Director

90

MATERIAL SUBMITTED FOR THE RECORD BY DAVID ANDREW WEINBERG, PH.D., SENIOR
FELLOW, FOUNDATION FOR DEFENSE OF DEMOCRACIES

MONUMENTAL FIGHT: COUNTERING THE ISLAMIC STATE'S ANTIQUITIES TRAFFICKING

BY YAYA J. FANUSIE AND ALEXANDER JOFFE
Center on Sanctions & Illicit Finance at Foundation for Defense of Democracies

EXECUTIVE SUMMARY

In the four and a half years since the Syrian civil war began, the terrorist group known as Islamic State (IS) has become one of the most destabilizing actors in the Middle East. Its growth is funded mainly through revenues from its well-documented seizure of oil fields,[1] but less understood is its trade in looted antiquities – a market fed largely by Western demand. Although the antiquities trade is considerably smaller than other elements of the IS financial portfolio, it offers the group the prospect of high mark-ups, global demand, a low likelihood for military disruption, and a willing pool of civilians who supply labor for the trade.

Assessing IS revenue from antiquities is difficult given the opaque nature of the black market, but official U.S. trade data indicate a 23-percent uptick in antiques leaving the Levant region since 2010. Islamic State's antiquities trafficking benefits from a global market, and goes hand-in-hand with its broader aim to purge society of pre- or non-Islamic influence. The group deals in antiquities by exerting state-like dominance, including a bureaucracy to control excavations and smuggling, and uses a variety of techniques to profit from pillaged artifacts. IS leverages the financial self-interest of civilian populations who locate and smuggle antiquities, but this reliance may become a weak point if policy efforts successfully stifle the underground market.

Combatting IS funding through antiquities trafficking will require a multi-pronged approach: leveraging national and international economic tools, creating new data collection and enforcement capabilities, and facilitating cooperation among public and private entities. Success

---

[1] "Where Islamic State Gets its Money," *The Economist*, January 4, 2015.
(http://www.economist.com/blogs/economist-explains/2015/01/economist-explains)

will mean not only depriving a brutal terrorist group of crucial funding, but also preserving the priceless relics of our past.

IS militants smashing antiquities at a Mosul museum.

INTRODUCTION

Islamic State operates over roughly half of the territory of Syria,[2] controls several major cities in Iraq,[3] and unleashes tactics of astonishing brutality on the populations under its control. It has been dubbed the world's richest terror army.[4] Unlike older internationally funded jihadist groups like al-Qaeda and state proxies like Hezbollah, IS generates enough revenue within the territory it controls to cover a payroll of hundreds of millions of dollars in its fighters' annual salaries.[5]

[2] Kareem Shaheen, "Isis Controls 50% of Syria' after Seizing Historic City of Palmyra," *The Guardian* (U.K.), May 21, 2015. (http://www.theguardian.com/world/2015/may/21/isis-palmyra-syria-islamic-state); Armin Rosen, "What Everyone is Missing About ISIS' Big Week," *Business Insider*, May 22, 2015. (http://www.businessinsider.com/isis-control-of-territory-2015-5)

[3] Christopher M. Blanchard, Carla E. Humud, Kenneth Katzman, & Matthew C. Weed, "The 'Islamic State' Crisis and U.S. Policy," Congressional Research Service, June 11, 2015. (http://fas.org/sgp/crs/midcast/R43612.pdf)

[4] "The World's Richest Terror Army," *BBC Two* (U.K.), April 22, 2015. (http://www.bbc.co.uk/programmes/b05s4ytp)

[5] Mirren Gidda, "ISIS is Facing a Cash Crunch in the Caliphate," *Newsweek*, September 23, 2015. (http://europe.newsweek.com/isis-are-facing-cash-crunch-caliphate-333422)

Islamic State is comprised of former Iraqi regime elements, foreign fighters, local tribes, and others who have sworn allegiance to the group for ideological reasons or simple fear. In its core regions of Syria and northern and western Iraq, IS has developed coherent, state-like bureaucratic structures. The group now supervises a broad array of everyday activities, including "tax forms for electricity services, licenses for excavations of antiquities, phone subscriptions, fees for sanitation services, agricultural crop plants, unified Friday sermons, vaccination programs, and fixing rent rates for property."[6] IS helps individuals open businesses while providing "medical, social, policing, and rescue services" as well as enforcing civil, criminal, and strict religious laws.[7]

Captured documentation suggests IS earns several million dollars per day from its diverse financial portfolio[8] – generally balancing its books and even running a surplus.[9] Oil remains the group's most important commodity, followed by theft, taxation, kidnapping and ransom, and extortion. The role of foreign funders – directly through cash or indirectly through Islamic charities – remains the subject of debate,[10] but one recent estimate suggests that in 2013 and 2014, IS earned some $40 million from Saudi, Kuwaiti, and Qatari donors.[11] IS often uses cash

---

[6] Aymenn al-Tamimi, "The Evolution in Islamic State Administration: The Documentary Evidence," *Perspectives on Terrorism*, 2015. (http://www.terrorismanalysts.com/pt/index.php/pot/article/view/447/html)

[7] Laith Alkhouri & Alex Kassirer, "Governing the Caliphate: The Islamic State Picture," *CTC Sentinel*, August 2015, page 18. (https://www.ctc.usma.edu/posts/governing-the-caliphate-the-islamic-state-picture): For context on ISIS see: Jessica Stern & J.M. Berger, *ISIS: The State of Terror*, (New York: Ecco, 2015), and Michael Weiss & Hassan Hassan, *ISIS: Inside the Army of Terror*, (New York: Regan Arts, 2015).

[8] Bryan Price, Dan Milton, Muhammad al-'Ubaydi, and Nelly Lahoud, "The Group That Calls Itself a State: Understanding the Evolution and Challenges of the Islamic State," *Combating Terrorism Center at West Point*, December 2014.

[9] Patrick B. Johnson, "Countering ISIL's Financing," *Testimony Before the Committee on Financial Services, United States House of Representatives*, November 13, 2014. (http://www.rand.org/pubs/testimonies/CT419.html); Charles Lister, "Cutting Off ISIS' Cash Flow," October 24, 2014.
(http://www.brookings.edu/blogs/markaz/posts/2014/10/24-lister-cutting-off-isis-jabhat-al-nusra-cash-flow)

[10] Janine Di Giovanni, Leah McGrath Goodman, and Damien Sharkov, "How Does ISIS Fund Its Reign of Terror?" *Newsweek*, November 6, 2014. (http://www.newsweek.com/2014/11/14/how-does-isis-fund-its-reign-terror-282607.html?piano_t=1); Carla E. Humud, Robert Pirog, & Liana Rosen, "Islamic State Financing and U.S. Policy Approaches," *Congressional Research Service*, April 10, 2015, page 11.

[11] U.S. Department of State, Overseas Security Advisory Council, "International Non-Military Measures Against ISIL," October 19, 2015, page 4. (http://freebeacon.com/wp-content/uploads/2015/10/ISIL.pdf)

to avoid leaving a trail of transactions while also exploiting the Qatari and Kuwaiti banking systems, which are less rigorous at monitoring transactions than their Saudi counterparts.[12]

One income stream in particular gives the group significant strategic advantages against existing counter-terror finance efforts: illegal antiquities. The main buyers are, ironically, history enthusiasts and art aficionados in the United States and Europe – representatives of the Western societies which IS has pledged to destroy. This poses several challenges to policy makers, as well as opportunities. This report explores the history of antiquity smuggling, details the way IS exploits this trade, and offers suggestions as to how Washington and its partners may stem the flow of this important financial stream to the world's most dangerous terrorist organization.

Historical Context

Antiquities theft has occurred since antiquity itself. Ancient Egyptian court cases include records of tomb robbing, and countless archaeological sites show signs of looting. Since antiquity, local profiteers have treated archaeological and heritage sites as resources to be mined – both for their man-made treasures and even for their nutrient-rich soil for use as fertilizer.

Starting in the Renaissance, Europeans in particular began to collect and trade antiquities, helping to preserve the Classical tradition of Greece and Rome. During the 19th century, the Mediterranean and the Middle East became focal points for individual and national European collections and museums, which competed to acquire, research, and display ancient artifacts.

That competition, increasingly tied to European imperialism, also spurred the development of scholarship on the ancient world. Egyptian hieroglyphic texts were first deciphered in 1822 on the basis of the Rosetta Stone, acquired in Egypt by Napoleon and later taken to London. The expansion of upper class and then middle class European tourism to these regions in the late 19th century expanded the market for artifacts further still.

---

[12] Janine Di Giovanni, Leah McGrath Goodman and Damien Sharkov, "How Does ISIS Fund Its Reign of Terror?" *Newsweek*, November 6, 2014. (http://www.newsweek.com/2014/11/14/how-does-isis-fund-its-reign-terror-282607.html?piano_t=1)

While official permission was required to excavate in the territory of the Ottoman Empire, antiquities markets were essentially unregulated until the emergence of independent nation-states; Egypt's first antiquities law was issued in 1835, while the Ottoman Antiquities Law dates to 1874.[13] Today, most states nominally regulate the ownership and excavation of antiquities, but regulations regarding the export of artifacts vary.

Looting by conquering armies is also as old as war itself, but the connection between antiquities theft, organized crime, and terrorism is of more recent vintage. The modern-day theft and resale of antiquities by organized crime networks is well documented,[14] and like any commodity, the antiquities market is driven by fluctuations in supply and demand. The relationship with terrorism is more recent still but difficult to isolate, as terror groups often work alongside organized crime networks.

The full version of this document can be viewed by going to:
http://cradmin.clerk.house.gov/repository/FA/FA18/20151117/104202/HHRG-114-FA18-20151117-SD001.pdf

---

[13] Morag M. Kersel, "The Changing Legal Landscape for Middle Eastern Archaeology in the Colonial Era, 1800-1930," in G. Emberling (ed.), *Pioneers to the Past: American Archaeologists in the Middle East 1919-1920* (Chicago: The Oriental Institute Museum Publications), pages 85-90. (http://traffickingculture.org/wp-content/uploads/2013/01/Kersel-2010-Changing-Legal-landscape-Pioneers-to-the-Past.pdf)

[14] Peter B. Campbell, "The Illicit Antiquities Trade as a Transnational Criminal Network: Characterizing and Anticipating Trafficking of Cultural Heritage," *International Journal of Cultural Property*, 20 (2013), pages 131-153. (http://journals.cambridge.org/action/displayAbstract?fromPage=online&aid=8937643&fileId=S0940739113000015)

MATERIAL SUBMITTED FOR THE RECORD BY THE HONORABLE TED POE, A REPRESENTATIVE IN CONGRESS FROM THE STATE OF TEXAS, AND CHAIRMAN, SUBCOMMITTEE ON TERRORISM, NONPROLIFERATION, AND TRADE

The Honorable Ted Poe
Chairman, Subcommittee on Terrorism, Non-Proliferation and Trade
The House Committee on Foreign Affairs
2170 Rayburn House Office Building
Washington, DC 20515

Dear Mr. Poe,

I write today in response to the November 17, 2015 subcommittee hearing on terrorist financing, specifically concerning the testimony and comments of Mrs. Diane Foley and specific attacks against me. The mother of a murdered son is entitled to our compassion for her loss, especially when her child is so brutally and publicly murdered as Jim Foley was. She is also entitled to a decent respect for her opinions, but she is not entitled to rewrite history to support a false narrative. While I remain heartbroken for the Foleys and other families whose loved ones were brutally murdered by the Islamic State and cannot begin to imagine their grief and sense of loss, I cannot remain silent in the face of her slanderous accounts of my interactions with her or the egregious misrepresentations regarding the U.S. Government's efforts to recover her son and others held captive by terrorist organizations.

Let me be clear: I categorically deny that I "threatened" Mrs. Foley and take strong exception to any suggestion that I impeded their attempts to bring Jim home. I also strongly disagree with her numerous, baseless assertions that: the families of hostages were "truly abandoned" by the United States Government (USG); that the USG "refused to engage at a high level with our allies" or "refused to engage with the French or UK to save our citizens;" that the US hostage policy "prohibited our government from interacting in any way with Jim's captors...even investigating who our son's captors were;" and that anyone had "specific information regarding the exact locations of their captivity beginning in the fall of 2013," much less that the USG failed to act on credible information failed to investigate and act on such information. All of these assertions are patently and demonstrably false; many more of her statements, assessments, and the conclusions and recommendations that flow from them are not just wrong but also harmful to our efforts to combat terrorism.

Background and Biographical Information

To help you understand why I would find her remarks so personally offensive and profoundly hypocritical, let me provide my professional background to help place my remarks in context. I served nearly 28 years as an infantry and Special Forces officer, retiring in May 2015. In the last year and half of that service, I served in the Counterterrorism Directorate at the National Security Council and chaired the Interagency Hostage and Personnel Recovery Working Group. I am a veteran of combat in the First Gulf War (aka Operation Desert Shield/Desert Storm), Operation Enduring Freedom in Afghanistan, and Operations Iraqi Freedom and New Dawn in Iraq. I was among the first group of U.S. soldiers on the ground in Afghanistan after the horrific events of September 11th and received our Nation's second highest decoration for valor, the Distinguished Service Cross, for my actions during the Battle of Qala-I Jangi in Mazar-e Sharif during the last week of November 2001. From 2003 through 2011, I set foot in Iraq every year and served multiple, extended tours, including commanding a joint unit of Army Green Berets, Navy SEALS, and Air Force Special Tactics units.

These deployments weren't just hard on me—they were hard on my wife (of 24 years) and two daughters. I have risked my own life on multiple occasions and buried friends and subordinates who have willingly sacrificed their own lives fighting terrorists, some of whom are now members of the Islamic State. I have personally witnessed much death and destruction caused by terrorists and know well the costs that we pay to combat terrorism. I take these efforts and my responsibilities seriously; I have always, in actions great and small, honored my oath "to support and defend the Constitution of the United States against all enemies, foreign and domestic."

Was there a Threat of Prosecution? No.

Mrs. Foley's has repeatedly said that I "threatened" her with prosecution three times—an accusation now a part of the Congressional Record. At no time did I "threaten" her or any of the families with prosecution. And, to bolster that fact, let me note that as a Director for Counterterrorism on the National Security Council, I was not in a position to make or influence prosecutorial decisions or to interfere in any ongoing investigation. The true situation is much more complex. Let me provide a few facts:

- Request for immunity for legal violations: At the request of the families of the hostages held in Syria, we met or spoke on several occasions to discuss efforts to recover their loved ones. During each meeting, *the discussion of ransom payments was initiated by the families.* Specifically, in June 2014, the families inquired about the possibility of and process for obtaining a waiver from the Department of Treasury and pre-emptive immunity from the Attorney General which would allow them to raise funds and pay a ransom without risk of prosecution or penalty for violating US law.

- US law and policy on ransoms: Consistent with long-standing policy and the advice provided by the Departments of Justice, Treasury, and State, I carefully explained the Islamic State had been designated as a Foreign Terrorist Organization by the Department of State. You do not have to be a lawyer to understand that raising and paying a ransom to such a designated foreign terrorist organization would, under any conceivable scenario, constitute provision of material support. Regardless of their heart-wrenching plight, by law neither I, nor any other U.S. government official, could assist them in violating or circumventing any of these duly passed laws. I also reminded them that I had taken an oath to "support and the defend the Constitution" and that the legislation prohibiting material support to designated terrorist organizations had been duly passed by Congress and signed into law by the President; I would not be party in any way to attempts to violate these laws. *I urged the families to contact their local U.S. Attorney if they wanted to discuss the topic further.*

- Confirmation from FBI and Family Attorneys: I was not the only one who provided such advice. The Federal Bureau of Investigation (FBI) participated in these conversations and responded along the same lines, noting the role that prosecutorial discretion could play in these circumstances. The families also acknowledged that their own legal counsels had also provided similar advice regarding the legality of attempts to raise funds or pay ransoms. Finally, the families' request for immunity from prosecution is *prima facie* evidence that they themselves understood that paying ransom would be illegal.

Why Wouldn't We Engage Partners? We did.

Mrs. Foley has also claimed that I "made it clear" that the USG would not engage allies for help, would not attempt to rescue hostages, and "planned to abandon" the hostages. These accusations are utterly false. Once again, let me respond with some of the actual facts:

- Engagement with Allies: From the very beginning, every part of the executive branch was continually engaging with our allies and partners on many different aspects of the Syrian hostage crisis. Our diplomatic, law enforcement, military, and intelligence communities regularly exchanged information with our allies and partners and sought assistance from their international counterparts—but only in ways consistent with our law, policy, and international agreements. These engagements with allies and partners, especially with the UK and France, were extensive and our requests for assistance were conveyed repeatedly in bilateral engagements at every level.

- Qatar: It is likely that Mrs. Foley's complaints about "engaging allies" relate specifically to our lack of engagement with Qatar in the resolution of the Syrian hostage crisis. Many of the families believed that Qatar held special influence over the captors and could successfully negotiate their release. Of course, Qatar was instrumental in the negotiations which freed Peter Theo Curtis in August 2014. However, Mr. Curtis was held by a group despised by the Islamic State (al Nusrah Front), and the details of how Qatar secured Mr. Curtis' release remain unknown. Qatar denied paying a ransom but would not disclose how they were able to secure his freedom. Personally, I find it incredible that al-Nusrah would release an American on humanitarian grounds and without substantial compensation. Given Qatar's apparent indifference to financing of terrorist organizations, as noted by multiple witnesses and members of the subcommittee, I consistently opposed any effort to enlist Qatar as an intermediary in these cases and consider my opposition to their involvement vindicated.

Why Didn't Law Enforcement Interview Other Released Hostages? They tried.

In her testimony and other public statements, Mrs. Foley has repeatedly maligned our law enforcement and intelligence professionals for failing to speak with released hostages, portraying them as incompetent and/or unconcerned. But this characterization studiously omits a very important fact: our law enforcement and intelligence professionals can only speak with these individuals with the permission of their government and their consent. Let me note just two of the constraints they faced:

- Host nation obstruction: Our embassies and other executive branch officials made immediate and repeated requests to speak with foreign citizens released by the Islamic State. However, as you might imagine, foreign governments that have just abrogated their international commitments to refrain from paying ransoms are not eager to cooperate fully with U.S. investigators. With very few exceptions, these governments obstructed official efforts to interview released hostages.

- Terrorist intimidation: Much is now known about the horrific physical and psychological violence that the Islamic State inflicted on its captives. Additionally, the captors threatened hostages with retaliation if they cooperated with law enforcement or intelligence agencies after their release. Moreover, even without the threats and intimidation, released hostages are understandably reluctant to speak about such traumatic and life-altering experiences. These real and substantial limitations were carefully explained to Mrs. Foley. Surely, she can empathize with some of these individuals and their families.

Why didn't they try to rescue the hostages? They did.

Mrs. Foley has claimed that the families possessed "specific information regarding the exact locations of captivity beginning in the fall of 2013" and that despite that, I had told them that the USG "would not conduct a military operation to rescue" the hostages. Let me clarify this in two ways—first in terms of timeline and then in terms of the type of "specific" information we need to actually conduct a rescue operation.

- Timeline: In the fall of 2013 nobody—not the families, their employers, private investigators, the USG, or any foreign government—had specific information on the identity of the hostage takers much less information regarding the exact location of the hostages. The hostage takers did not contact the Foley family until December 2013 and went to great lengths to conceal their identity and location.

- Specificity: During the May 2014 meetings with families, they presented information about potential "locations." Some of the information had been provided directly to Mrs. Foley by released foreign hostages but, unfortunately, the information was fragmentary and outdated. For instance, the purported location of the hostages was "Aleppo." While such information may be useful for some purposes, it is certainly not sufficient to enable or justify a rescue operation. As an experienced Special Forces officer, I explained that highly detailed intelligence is necessary to conduct a hostage rescue operation, especially in a conflict zone like Syria. This information is needed for the safety of the hostages and the rescue force; it enables the rescue force to reach the hostages rapidly and overwhelm guards before they can harm hostages. I carefully explained that the information they provided did not meet that threshold but that we would incorporate it into our intelligence analysis. I did not, and would never, categorically rule out rescue operations.

As we now know, President Obama authorized and the Department of Defense executed an extremely high-risk rescue operation near the heart of the Islamic State in early July 2014. The intelligence that enabled the operation was the result of extensive coordination among the U.S. intelligence, law enforcement, diplomatic, and military communities and with some of our key allies. It represented the culmination of thousands upon thousands of man-hours across the FBI, CIA, NSA, DIA, NGA, NRO, NCTC, DOS, DOJ and DOD. Sadly, the hostages had been moved and the rescue attempt was unsuccessful but it was not for lack of effort and prioritization.

Why didn't U.S. officials interact with the captors? We cannot and should not.

Mrs. Foley has lamented the fact that the U.S. Government would not engage in direct communications with the hostage takers—a statement that is undeniably true. She has further alleged that this lack of direct engagement with the captors prevented the government form investigating the identity of the captors—a statement that is categorically false. I would like to add some important context to this important topic:

- A substantive concession: The United States cannot and should not engage in direct communications with terrorist organizations like the Islamic State. To do so would be would be as unhelpful as it is unwise. Direct communications would themselves be a substantive concession to the Islamic State, granting implicit recognition to them as something more than a criminal organization. There is nothing that we can negotiate and such would undoubtedly exploit this recognition in their voluminous propaganda. It would also raise expectations that, like France or Italy or Germany, the United States Government itself would provide a ransom. Finally, and most importantly, it would create powerful incentives to kidnap American citizens leading to both increased numbers of kidnappings and increased pressure to pay ransoms.

- Unnecessary: The United States has an extensive variety of intelligence gathering capabilities. It simply does not need to engage in direct communications with the Islamic State to gather intelligence about the identity of the captors.

Concerns about current Hostage Policy

I would like to comment also on recent decision to permit families of hostages to pay ransom to terrorist organizations without fear of prosecution, regardless of any legal prohibitions to such payments. Paying ransom is not wrong because it is against the law; it is against the law because it is wrong.

- Funds terrorist organizations: It directly abets and aids a criminal and evil enterprise—one that United States has spent thousands of lives and billions of dollars to combat. This policy rewards the terrorist's criminal behavior and funds other terrorist activities, whether it is training, recruitment, attacks, or further kidnappings. Moreover, allowing families to pay ransom is precisely the type of emotional response that terrorists seek when they take hostages.

- Encourages more kidnapping: Ransoms are also a bad policy if you are trying to combat kidnapping for ransom. Simply put, paying ransom is likely to lead to more frequent kidnappings. A secondary effect is the moral hazard such a policy creates for citizens travelling to high risk areas by potentially mitigating the risk of kidnapping. Even if the ability to pay ransom is not dispositive for all potential travelers, it is bound to encourage some potential travelers to take the risk, increasing the number of kidnapping targets.

- Harms international counterterrorism efforts: The United States, along with its allies in the United Kingdom, has taken an aggressive and leading role in these efforts, especially the scourge of kidnapping-for-ransom (KFR). Multiple United Nations Security Council Resolutions have reinforced the necessity of combating terrorist financing and a 2013 joint communique from the G8 obligated all members to "unequivocally reject the payment of ransoms to terrorists." Yet, this new policy not only allows payment of ransoms but encourages it by removing carefully erected barriers and making payment of ransom insurance policies much simpler. This ill-conceived policy shift will not only make American citizens more enticing targets but also significantly undermine U.S. credibility as it seeks to end European ransom payments.

- Undermines a commitment to the rule of law: The Department of Justice is placing terrorist financing and material support offenses at the center of efforts to counter suspected Islamic State sympathizers and recruits in the United States. At the same time the Obama Administration is prosecuting some citizens for purchasing airline tickets to Turkey, ostensibly with the intent to fight alongside the Islamic State, it is also promising to allow other American citizens to potentially transfer millions of dollars to the Islamic State, without fear of prosecution. Such fiat goes beyond simple prosecutorial discretion and effectively grants certain families (those with financial means or connections to deep-pocketed individuals) pre-emptive immunity from laws designed to prevent material support of terrorism. This makes a mockery of the claim that we are a "Nation of laws" and is a disservice to all who have risked their lives to combat terrorism.

- **Exposes families of hostages to further exploitation:** Kidnapping imposes a cruel burden on the families and victimizes them in multiple ways. And while the revised policy stems from an admirable desire to avoid adding to the pain of already suffering families, it strips them of a very useful defense and bargaining tool in the face of terrorist demands for multi-million dollar ransoms. The Islamic State and al Qa'ida clearly follow our domestic political developments and will doubtlessly seek to exploit this new policy. In the absence of any threat of prosecution, terrorists will relentlessly demand that families beggar themselves to pay the ransom.

As the number of attacks and fatalities from terrorism continue to increase, it is clear that the United States and the rest of the civilized world faces an increasingly difficult challenge in their ongoing effort to combat the Islamic State and al-Qa'ida. Kidnapping for ransom is a terrible crime that is difficult to combat even in the best of circumstances. Let's not make these challenges any more difficult by allowing ransom payments.

I respectfully request that this letter be entered into the record of the subcommittee hearing on November 17, 2015. I am available to you, your personal staff, other committee members, or professional staff to discuss any aspect of this letter or events recounted herein.

Sincerely,

Mark E. Mitchell
Colonel (Retired), U.S. Army

Made in the USA
Middletown, DE
27 June 2017